OCCASIONAL PAPER 206

The Dominican Republic
Stabilization, Reform, and Growth

By a Staff Team led by Philip Young
and comprising

Jaime Cardoso
David Dunn
Alessandro Giustiniani
Werner Keller
Jimmy McHugh
Francisco Nadal-De Simone
John Panzer
Randa Sab
Raimundo Soto
Evan Tanner

INTERNATIONAL MONETARY FUND
Washington DC
2001

© 2001 International Monetary Fund

Production: IMF Graphics Section
Charts: Sanaa Elaroussi
Typesetting: UpperCase Publication Services, Ltd.

Library of Congress Cataloging-in-Publication Data

The Dominican Republic : stabilization, reform, and growth / by a staff team
led by Philip Young and comprising Jaime Cardoso . . . [et al.].

     p.   cm. — (Occasional paper ; 206)

    Includes bibliographical references.

    ISBN 1-58906-046-6

    1. Dominican Republic—Economic policy. 2. Dominican Republic—
Economic conditions—1961- I. Young, Philip M. II. Cardoso, Jaime. III.
Occasional paper (International Monetary Fund) ; 206.
HC153.5 .D662   2001
338.97293—dc21   2001039780

Price: US$20.00
(US$17.50 to full-time faculty members and
students at universities and colleges)

Please send orders to:
International Monetary Fund, Publication Services
700 19th Street, N.W., Washington, D.C. 20431, U.S.A.
Tel.: (202) 623-7430   Telefax: (202) 623-7201
E-mail: publications@imf.org
Internet: http://www.imf.org

recycled paper

Contents

Figures

The following symbols have been used throughout this paper:

. . . to indicate that data are not available;

— to indicate that the figure is zero or less than half the final digit shown, or that the item does not exist;

– between years or months (e.g., 1998–99 or January–June) to indicate the years or months covered, including the beginning and ending years or months;

/ between years (e.g., 1998/99) to indicate a fiscal (financial) year.

"Billion" means a thousand million.

Minor discrepancies between constituent figures and totals are due to rounding.

The term "country," as used in this paper, does not in all cases refer to a territorial entity that is a state as understood by international law and practice; the term also covers some territorial entities that are not states, but for which statistical data are maintained and provided internationally on a separate and independent basis.

List of Abbreviations

ACP	African, Caribbean, and Pacific countries
ACS	Association of Caribbean States
BCRD	Central Bank of the Dominican Republic
CAFTA	Central American Free Trade Area
CARICOM	Caribbean Community
CCC	U.S. Commodity Credit Corporation
CDE	*Companía Dominicana de Electricidad*
CEA	*Consejo Estatal del Azúcar*
CREP	*Comisión de Reforma de la Empresa Pública*
DGII	*Dirección General de Impuestos Internos*
EMP	exchange market pressure
EU	European Union
FTAA	Free Trade Area of the Americas
FTZ	free-trade zones
IDB	Inter-American Development Bank
LAC	Latin American countries
LIBOR	London interbank offered rate
NAFTA	North American Free Trade Agreement
OLS	Ordinary least squares
ONAPLAN	*Oficina Nacional de Planeamiento*
ONAPRE	*Oficina Nacional de Presupuesto*
OPEC	Organization of Petroleum Exporting Countries
TFP	total factor productivity
WTO	World Trade Organization

Preface

Most of the material presented in this Occasional Paper was originally prepared as background for discussions in the IMF Executive Board. It has been updated to take account of developments through early 2001. The authors are grateful to the Dominican authorities for extensive discussions and comments and for their assistance in providing data and other source material.

This Occasional Paper has benefited from the comments of staff in the Western Hemisphere Department as well as the Latin American and Caribbean Region of the World Bank. In particular, the authors would like to thank Patricia Brenner, Eliot Kalter, Saul Lizondo, and Robert Rennhack for their valuable comments. John Panzer works for the World Bank and Raimundo Soto is with the Instituto de Economía, Pontificia Universidad Católica de Chile.

The authors would also like to express their appreciation for the valuable research assistance that was provided by Branko Maric, formerly of the Western Hemisphere Department. Lucy Ulrich of the IMF's External Relations Department edited the report and coordinated its production for publication.

The opinions expressed are solely those of the authors and do not necessarily reflect the views of the IMF, Executive Directors, or the authorities of the Dominican Republic.

Overview

This Occasional Paper is a compilation of papers that are linked by a common theme—stabilization, structural reform, and economic growth in the Dominican Republic. The papers summarize the authorities' stabilization efforts, how these efforts were subsequently reinforced by certain key structural reforms, and other related developments that help explain the remarkable performance of the Dominican Republic's economy in the 1990s during which the country achieved one of the highest output growth rates in Latin America, combined with low inflation, and a much improved external debt profile. The performance is all the more striking when contrasted with the severe imbalances of the previous decade—one of widening external current account and public sector deficits, accelerating inflation, and declining growth.

As a result of these imbalances, by the end of the 1980s, pressures on the balance of payments and prices had reached unsustainable levels. The government suspended certain external debt-service payments, giving rise to large external payments arrears. Conditions deteriorated to such an extent that a drastic reorientation of policies was urgently needed. This is the setting for Chapter I, *Stabilization and Structural Reforms,* which describes the authorities' structural reform efforts in the 1990s. The lesson that emerges is that a great deal was accomplished on the structural front, which contributed fundamentally to the extended period of growth observed in the 1990s. The administration of President Hipólito Mejía has continued, if not accelerated, the reform momentum, with the approval of a new hydrocarbons law (removing administration discretion from the setting of domestic fuels prices), substantially reducing the average external tariff rate, and increasing consumption taxes to encourage saving and provide the needed resources for priority social expenditures. Nonetheless, a comprehensive reform agenda (much of which is currently being considered by congress) lies ahead. It includes modernization of the public administration, improving the transparency of economic policies, and strengthening the supervisory and regulatory framework of the financial system.

During the 1980s, in order to protect domestic industries, the authorities often resorted to trade-restricting measures. This resulted in a highly protected domestic industry, which was ill-prepared to enter an increasingly competitive world market. Recognizing that domestic firms risked being unable to keep pace with international conglomerates, the authorities have embarked on a trade reform program. Chapter II, *Trade Reform Continues,* provides a history of these reforms, which form an integral part of the structural reform agenda. The restrictiveness of the trade regime has been diminishing—for example, congress recently approved several regional trade agreements, lowered tariffs further in 2001, and plans additional reductions in coming years—and this is leading to a harmonization of the Dominican Republic's trade policies with those of its neighbors.

The authorities often resorted to external arrears as a means of financing the external current account deficits of the 1980s. Although rescheduling agreements were reached with the international banking community and with the Paris Club of official creditors in the mid-1980s, they met with limited success until the authorities embarked on their stabilization program of the early 1990s. Chapter III, *Successful External Debt Restructuring,* gives an overview of these developments and highlights the improvement in the external debt profile in recent years.

The deepening fiscal imbalances of the 1980s, largely financed domestically, but also with external arrears, led to rapidly accelerating inflation. The economic system was at risk of collapse and it needed a rapid and substantial fiscal adjustment. In just one year, the consolidated public sector balance turned from a deficit of more than 3 percent of GDP in 1990 to near balance in the following year. The underlying theme of Chapter IV, *A Review of Fiscal Policy During the 1990s and Current Policy Considerations,* is that the subsequent maintenance of fiscal discipline over a number of years has been a key factor behind the exemplary performance of the Dominican economy. The chapter includes a discussion of the major tax reforms and improvements in administration that were implemented during the 1990s, as well as developments in expenditure policy. It concludes with a look ahead to the recently initiated Integrated Financial Management Program, which is expected to yield substantial benefits in terms of transparency and rationalization of the fiscal accounts.

Chapter V, *Capital Accumulation, Total Factor Productivity, and Growth,* considers trends in capital accumulation, technological change, and economic growth. The restoration of macroeconomic stability and the initiation of structural reforms coincided with strong economic growth and poverty reduction. The chapter shows that this growth was anchored by a resurgence of capital formation and strong productivity growth. Sustaining high economic growth rates requires continuous efforts in fostering investment and productivity growth. This in turn will necessitate continued structural reforms and investment in health and education, the types of investment that help to "crowd in" rather than "crowd out" private sector investment.

In addition to the chapters described above, this paper also includes two technical papers, Chapters VI and VII. The first provides an empirical estimation of money demand in the Dominican Republic. Real money balances are found to be cointegrated with real GDP and interest rates. In the short run, changes in opportunity cost variables (including either domestic interest rates or the *differential* between domestic and U.S. interest rates) also help explain changes in real money balances. The strength of this relationship holds up over time when money is defined as M2. It dissipates over time, however, when money is measured as M1 (that is, the long-run coefficient is not statistically significant). In the second paper, monetary and exchange rate policies (including reserve movements) are combined in a model of exchange market pressure defined as the sum of exchange rate depreciation and the outflow of official reserves. Consistent with a stable money demand, a reduction in domestic credit results in a decline in the exchange market pressure index. Thus, contractionary monetary policy can be effective in raising official reserves.

I   Stabilization and Structural Reforms

Since 1992, the Dominican Republic has experienced an extended period of robust economic growth, declining unemployment rates, modest consumer price inflation, and a generally manageable external position. Indeed, in the second half of the 1990s, the Dominican Republic ranked among the world's fastest-growing economies, with particularly strong performances in the telecommunications, construction, free-trade zone, and tourism sectors.

This picture contrasts dramatically with the country's economic performance during the 1980s, when the combination of severe monetary and fiscal imbalances, pervasive price controls, financial sector rigidities, multiple currency practices, and an extremely restrictive trade regime resulted in acute economic distortions and an inability to manage adverse shocks to the economy. External deficits soared, the peso was sharply devalued several times, and the government incurred external arrears. Moreover, economic activity stagnated.

The turnaround was accomplished through an impressive and wide-ranging stabilization and structural adjustment effort initiated during 1990–92. This program permanently changed the economy's growth path, although individual elements met varying degrees of success. Domestic imbalances were addressed through measures aimed at strengthening public finances, improving monetary control, and reducing distortions in financial markets. Many restrictions that plagued the exchange and trade regime were removed, fostering the integration of the Dominican Republic into the world economy.

Despite the fragile political situation following the 1994 and 1996 presidential elections, the Dominican authorities succeeded in maintaining a broadly stable macroeconomic framework, although the pace of structural reform slowed somewhat. More recently, momentum appears to have picked up again, with the passage of the new hydrocarbons law, private capitalization of several public enterprises, reform of the tax code, and a reduction in tariff barriers. To lead the economy into the new millennium, the government has a broad agenda of other important structural reforms, including improving social sector policies, modernizing the public administration, increasing the transparency of economic and financial policies, and strengthening the soundness and stability of the financial system.

The Lost Decade: 1981–90

As with most of Latin America, the 1980s was a period of economic turmoil for the Dominican Republic. Economic rigidities and policy inconsistencies prolonged the country's difficulties. Large fiscal deficits contributed to excessive monetary expansion and inflationary pressures, which in turn exacerbated the distortions created by extensive price controls. An overvalued domestic currency and multiple exchange rates, combined with extensive foreign exchange surrender requirements and high trade barriers, stifled export growth and foreign investment, while protecting inefficient domestic industries. Caps on interest rates and controls on credit allocation contributed to financial disintermediation and a general weakening of the financial system. Moreover, the central bank was steadily losing official reserves, and payments arrears on the public sector's external debt-service obligations were accumulating. Attempts to implement stabilization programs were short-lived, especially because of a lack of fiscal discipline.[1]

A number of structural weaknesses contributed to the severe fiscal imbalances. The consolidated public sector deficit[2] averaged over 5 percent of GDP between 1981 and 1990 (Table 1). Several factors contributed to this weak fiscal performance. First, the level of government revenues was low and volatile

---

[1]The intensity of the imbalances prompted recourse to IMF assistance in 1983 and 1985.

[2]This measure of the fiscal deficit includes the central bank's quasi-fiscal operational losses. These losses arise, in part, from operations associated with the intermediation of foreign loans to finance priority activities, the servicing of debt on behalf of the government, the financing of certain public enterprises, and payments to institutions being liquidated.

Table 1. Main Macroeconomic Indicators

	1981–85	1986–90	1991–95	1996–2000
	(Annual percent changes, averages)			
Real GDP	1.9	2.9	4.2	7.7
Real GDP per capita	−1.3	0.9	2.5	5.4
Consumer prices (during the period)	18.0	39.5	7.9	6.9
Money and quasi-money (M2)	16.5	43.2	22.6	20.1
	(In percent of GDP, averages)			
Consolidated public sector balance[1]	−5.4	−5.4	−1.2	−2.2
Consolidated public sector primary balance	−3.8	−3.3	0.5	−1.2
Inflation tax[2]	1.7	4.3	0.9	0.8
External current account balance	−3.7	−3.7	−3.9	−2.7
Foreign direct investment	0.6	1.6	2.2	−3.1
External debt (end-period)	64.7	72.2	33.0	18.6
External debt service	7.5	9.2	4.2	2.6

Sources: Central Bank of the Dominican Republic (BCRD); and IMF staff estimates.

[1]Includes quasi-fiscal losses of the central bank. Since this information is not available for the 1990–93 period, the central bank's losses are assumed to be zero for those years.

[2]The inflation tax is calculated as CPI inflation during the year times the stock of base money at the end of the previous year.

because of the strong dependence on international trade taxes and weak tax administration.[3] Second, public spending was highly discretionary and inflated by sizable losses of public enterprises, large increases in wages and employment, and excessive public investment programs. Finally, the implementation of corrective measures frequently lacked effectiveness and continuity.[4]

Large and persistent fiscal deficits represented a significant burden for monetary policy. While at the beginning of the decade more than half of the public deficit was financed by foreign loans, episodes of default on external and domestic government debt led to a progressive drying up of these sources of financing. This resulted in an increasing monetization of the overall public deficit, which in turn fueled inflationary and exchange rate pressures. The inflation tax, which averaged about ½ percent of GDP in 1981–83, surged to an average of about 3 percent of GDP for the rest of the decade.

Financial repression hampered the formation of savings and their productive allocation. With the aim of preserving financial equilibrium, although pursu-

ing conflicting policy objectives, the government tried to maintain tight control over the financial sector. Ceilings imposed on lending rates, high and differentiated reserve requirements, extensive financial restrictions, and the allocation of credit according to political priorities created a highly inefficient and distorted financial system that adversely affected the formation of domestic savings. At the same time, these restrictions led to the emergence of an active informal financial market, complicating control of monetary aggregates.

The limited degree of openness perpetuated domestic distortions. A system of multiple currency practices, foreign exchange restrictions, surrender requirements, import prohibitions, high import duties with discretionary exemptions, and export controls contributed to perpetuating distortions in domestic markets and undermined the development of the export sector.[5] Inconsistency between exchange rate policy and the stance of financial policies generated overvaluations of the peso that resulted in sizable devaluations in 1984, 1988, and in 1990.

As a result of these rigidities, economic performance was poor. Over the whole period, economic activity expanded at a slow pace (Figure 1) and per capita output was stagnant. Consumer price inflation, which was below 10 percent in the early 1980s, increased rapidly, reaching almost 80 percent by 1990. External current account deficits averaged about 4 percent of GDP. The uncertain economic environment

---

[3]In 1981–90, taxes on international trade and transactions averaged about 5 percent of GDP, representing more than one-third of central government revenues. In 1991–2000, taking into account the increase in foreign exchange commission in 1999–2000, the proceeds of these taxes amounted to about 4½ percent of GDP, equivalent to less than one-third of total revenues.

[4]For example, the effectiveness of introducing a value-added tax (VAT) in 1983 was curtailed by administrative resolutions that limited the tax base.

[5]For more details on external developments, see Chapter II.

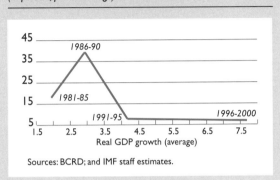

Figure 1. Scatter Diagram of Real GDP Growth Rates and Inflation Rates
(In percent, period average)

Sources: BCRD; and IMF staff estimates.

hindered inflows of foreign direct investment and caused a rapid accumulation of external debt. Despite some debt relief from official bilateral creditors in the mid-1980s, persistent large balance of payments deficits were financed through a rundown of official reserves and a buildup of payments arrears.[6]

The Initial Phase of the Reform Effort: 1991–95

In 1990, the economic situation deteriorated markedly owing to a preelectoral loosening of financial policies, a sharp deterioration of the terms of trade, and a prolonged drought.[7] Economic activity weakened, inflation accelerated, the balance of payments deficit widened, pressures on the exchange rate intensified, and external arrears increased, including those owed to the IMF, the World Bank, and the Inter-American Development Bank (IDB). When the government of President Joaquín Balaguer received a new mandate in August 1990, it embarked on a comprehensive economic program—known as the New Economic Program—that included price liberalization, fiscal consolidation, devaluation of the exchange rate, and decontrol of interest rates. Significant progress was made in normalizing relations with external creditors.[8] Although the reforms implemented in the early 1990s were substantial, several important distortions and policy weaknesses remained.

Fiscal consolidation lay at the heart of the New Economic Program. During 1990, the prices of a wide range of public sector goods and services were corrected to better reflect opportunity costs. In particular, the significant correction in the prices of petroleum products led to a remarkable increase in fuel tax revenues. The use of a market-determined exchange rate to calculate import duties boosted custom receipts.[9] A tax reform, approved in 1992, modified the income tax, converted all excise taxes from specific to value-based, broadened value-added tax (VAT), and raised its rate from 6 percent to 8 percent.[10] On the expenditure side, food subsidies were largely removed in 1990. Current and capital outlays were restrained during the early 1990s, mainly through strict application of a daily cash management system, particularly for special funds managed by the presidency. These measures shifted the public sector primary balance from a deficit of about 5 percent of GDP in 1989 to a surplus of close to 2 percent of GDP in 1991–92. Despite some recovery of government expenditures in the following years, especially capital expenditures, which had suffered the brunt of the earlier adjustment, the consolidated public sector deficit was contained at less than 1½ percent of GDP on average during 1991–95.[11]

To curb inflation, monetary conditions were tightened and monetary policy was made more effective. Lending and deposit rates were liberalized, rising to high positive levels in real terms. Reserve requirements, freezes on excess reserves, and credit ceilings continued to be the main instruments of monetary policy. The central bank started moving toward a more market-oriented management of domestic liquidity, however, by issuing its own certificates to increase reliance on open market operations.

The government put in place major reforms to the banking system to strengthen the financial system and eliminate distortions in credit markets. In late 1991, the structure of reserve requirements for commercial banks was unified at 20 percent for all deposits and selective portfolio requirements were abolished.[12] Furthermore, beginning in 1993, significant progress was made in developing banking

---

[6]At the end of 1990, the Dominican Republic's outstanding public external debt was about US$4.5 billion (some 72 percent of GDP), of which about US$1.5 billion was overdue.

[7]During 1989–90, while oil prices were increasing, prices of ferronickel, the country's main export item, were declining. This negatively affected government revenues.

[8]The government's stabilization and reform efforts were supported by an IMF Stand-By Arrangement, approved in August 1991 and extended in July 1993.

[9]Initially, import duties continued to be calculated at an exchange rate somewhat more appreciated than the market rate. In mid-1991, the authorities started to use the market exchange rate for this purpose.

[10]For more details on fiscal developments, see Chapter IV.

[11]This figure partially underestimates the actual consolidated public sector deficit because data on the central bank's quasi-fiscal losses are not available for 1990–93.

[12]While the basic reserve requirement has been unchanged since 1991, the authorities have continued to impose temporary reserve requirements in moments of particular tension in the money and exchange rate markets. Until recently, dollar deposits were only subject to reserve requirements when they exceeded three times capital. Currently, they are all subject to a reserve requirement of 10 percent.

supervision and prudential regulation. The Superintendency of Banks was restructured and modernized, norms on capital requirements were reviewed along the lines of the Basel agreement, rules on provisioning were clarified to ensure their enforcement, and limits on lending were established to minimize concentration risk. A draft Monetary and Financial Code was presented to congress to reform the statute of the central bank, strengthen banking supervision, and promote competition in the financial system. Enforcement of the new prudential regulations brought to light the weaknesses of the financial system. Insolvencies led the central bank to intervene in support of troubled institutions[13] and a number of banks were either merged or liquidated.

Significant measures were adopted to enhance the outward orientation of the Dominican economy. With the tax reform of September 1990, a gradual opening to external competition began. The level, numbers, and dispersion of tariff rates were reduced; the scope of exemptions was narrowed; and all import quotas and licensing agreements were eliminated, except for certain agricultural products. In January 1991, the multiple exchange rate was discontinued, and the "unified" official rate was set in relation to the commercial banks' exchange rate. Although the central bank continued to intervene in the foreign exchange market, a spread between the two rates emerged on numerous occasions. A requirement to surrender foreign exchange to the central bank remained in effect for certain transactions, but the scope of this requirement was reduced and an increasing number of transactions were conducted through the interbank market. A new Foreign Investment Law, approved in November 1995, opened up key sectors, including the banking sector, to foreign investment, extended to foreign participants the guarantees granted to domestic investors, and eliminated all restrictions on profit remittances and capital repatriation.

The response to the stabilization program was positive. Economic growth resumed, driven especially by those sectors that were more open to competition, such as tourism and tourism-related activities, construction, nonsugar manufacturing, and telecommunications. During 1991–95, the average rate of GDP growth accelerated to more than 4 percent, while inflation slowed sharply. Between the end of 1990 and the end of 1991, the 12-month change in consumer prices fell from 80 percent to 8 percent. Since then, inflation has remained in single digits, except in 1994, an election year. External imbalances were generally contained, except in 1992–93.[14] The improving economic situation meant the Dominican Republic began to attract sizable amounts of foreign direct investment, which became a steady source of financing for current account deficits. Various rescheduling and refinancing agreements with official and private creditors further relieved the external liquidity constraint.[15] This contributed to a steady and significant decline of the public external debt, which, between 1990 and 1995, more than halved from 72 percent to 33 percent of GDP.

Economic instability resumed in the run-up to the 1994 presidential election. Fiscal and monetary policies were relaxed, inflation rose, official foreign exchange reserves declined, and the spread between the official and the market exchange rates widened. The results of the presidential election were controversial. Ultimately, the political parties reached an agreement to shorten the presidential mandate and to hold a new election in 1996. During this interim period, the government resumed its efforts at stabilization. Although it lacked sufficient political support to implement a wide-ranging stabilization and reform program, the government avoided reversals of earlier reforms and was generally successful at containing economic imbalances.

A New Beginning: 1996–2000

A significant acceleration of the pace of economic growth, together with contained inflation, has characterized the second half of the 1990s. Since 1996, the Dominican Republic has ranked among the world's fastest-growing economies. The effects of past reforms and the sizable inflow of foreign direct investment are among the main factors to have contributed to this result. Unlike past episodes, this period of robust expansion has not been accompanied by a rekindling of inflationary pressures. Even in the months following Hurricane Georges, which hit the island in September 1998, 12-month inflation remained in single digits.

---

[13]Given the absence of institutional arrangements to protect small depositors, the central bank typically took over the assets and liabilities of financial institutions being liquidated. Initially, only small deposits were paid in cash while large deposits were exchanged for central bank certificates with a one-year maturity. Since September 1994, all deposits of liquidated banks have been converted into certificates with maturities ranging from six months to four years, depending on the size of the deposit. The certificates bear an interest rate of 10 percent a year.

[14]In those two years the current account deficit widened to nearly 8 percent and 5½ percent of GDP, respectively, partially reflecting a sharp increase in imports associated with the rapid expansion of the economy in 1992 (8 percent) and a decline in some traditional exports.

[15]Agreements on debt restructuring were reached with Paris Club creditors in November 1991 and with commercial banks in February 1994. Bilateral agreements were also signed with a number of countries, including Mexico and Venezuela. For more detail, see Chapter III.

Prudent fiscal and monetary policies were behind these achievements. Despite an increase in government noninterest current spending, the consolidated fiscal deficit remained relatively modest because of the rise in tax revenues stemming from a generalized improvement in tax enforcement and administration. More recently, fiscal policy slippages emerged in the second half of 1999, reflecting preelection-year expenditure overruns and a sharp fall in domestic fuel tax proceeds (the so-called oil differential tax) when domestic fuel prices were not adjusted in line with rising international oil prices.

The ensuing loss of international reserves and foreseen revenue losses associated with a planned reduction in external tariffs led the administration of President Hipólito Mejía[16] to adopt a number of corrective measures, including an increase in the VAT rate from 8 percent to 12 percent and a new hydrocarbon law that ended administrative discretion in the determination of retail prices. The conduct of monetary policy, however, continued to be hampered by limited central bank autonomy and the pursuit of potentially inconsistent objectives (that is, growth, inflation, interest rates, exchange rate, official reserves). In 2000, broad money growth was contained and positive real interest rates were maintained, although at times prior to August 2000 the central bank relied on direct instruments of monetary control, especially when exchange rate pressures emerged. Strengthening prudential regulation and banking supervision remained a top priority of the monetary authorities. With transactions in foreign currency rising, the authorities have taken a number of measures since 1998 to improve monitoring of exchange rate exposure and prevent excessive foreign borrowing. The measures include a limit of 30 percent of capital plus reserves on banks' short-term borrowing abroad, a 10 percent reserve requirement on deposits in foreign currency, and compulsory pre-approval by the central bank of all financial guarantees for foreign currency operations. However, a lack of political consensus has further delayed approval of the Monetary and Financial Code.

Public enterprise reform has gathered momentum recently. The Public Enterprise Reform Law, approved in June 1997, authorized more private sector participation in some productive areas still dominated by state-owned enterprises, such as the electricity and sugar sectors.[17] In early 1999, the state-owned flour mill (*Molinos Dominicanos*) was sold to the private sector. This was followed in April and May 1999 by the private capitalization of the distribution and gen-eration units of the state-owned electricity company.[18] In the second half of the year, the mills of the state-owned sugar company (*Consejo Estatal del Azúcar*—CEA) were leased, the state tobacco company was privately capitalized, and congress approved a 20-year concession for four international airports.

The results of trade liberalization have been mixed. While an ambitious trade reform bill was rejected by congress in 1996, further steps were made in reducing the restrictiveness of the trade regime. During 1998, a number of nontariff barriers were removed and free trade agreements were signed with the Central American Free Trade Area (CAFTA) and the Caribbean Community (CARICOM). Finally, in December 2000, congress approved tariff reform legislation that reduces the number of tariff bands to five from nine and lowers tariff rates, providing new momentum to the integration of the Dominican Republic into the world economy. The trade agreements with CARICOM and the CAFTA were approved in February and April 2001, respectively.

The Challenges Ahead

There is a need to press ahead with the reform agenda, which is broad and well articulated. In order to sustain a rapid pace of economic growth and development, the benefits of previous reforms need to be reinforced with fresh efforts: from enhancing economic policy transparency and good governance to strengthening the efficiency of public administration, and from further deepening of the financial sector to enhancing competition in the markets for goods and services. As shown in Table 2, important draft legislation is still under consideration by congress.

A key challenge is more transparent policymaking. Transparency promotes policy discipline and good governance, contributing to better economic performance.[19] To enhance fiscal credibility and permit a comprehensive assessment of the government's financial position, it is crucial to improve transparency in its operations, especially the execution and control of government expenditure.[20] The central bank

---

[16]President Mejía came to office in August 2000.

[17]This law also established the Commission for the Reform of Public Enterprises (*Comisión de Reforma de la Empresa Pública* —CREP), which is responsible for managing the reform and transformation of state-owned enterprises.

[18]Although the private capitalization of CDE was a crucial step forward, improvements in the electricity sector as well as in the power supply have been slower than expected because of the lack of a well-established legal and regulatory framework, insufficient competition in the wholesale market, and a deteriorating transmission infrastructure.

[19]On the issue of governance in the Dominican Republic, see Appendix I. Kopits and Craig (1998) provide a broad overview of many aspects of transparency in government operations.

[20]The government recently initiated an integrated financial management program, with financial support from the IDB, with the aim of enhancing transparency and accountability in the budget process.

needs to be given more autonomy to improve transparency in monetary operations and, as is already happening, increase its reliance on indirect monetary instruments. Full unification of the exchange markets would also eliminate an important impediment to efficient resource allocation. Together with the

Table 2. Structural Reforms

Reform	Description	Status
Privatization/Capitalization		
Dominican Electricity Co.	Create a joint venture; 50 percent state-owned and 50 percent private	Completed in May 1999
State Tobacco Co.	Create a joint venture; 50 percent state-owned and 50 percent private	Completed in January 2000
State Sugar Co.	Lease sugar mills to private sector	Completed in September 1999
Salt and gypsum mines	Create a joint venture; 50 percent state-owned and 50 percent private	Completed in May 2000
Gold mine	Lease mines to private sector	Invited bidding for the Rosario Dominicana mine in November 2000
Dominican Painting Co., Paper Industry, Dominican Aviation Co.	Create a joint venture; 50 percent state-owned and 50 percent private	Capitalization process suspended. Bidding will restart in June 2001
State-owned free-trade zone parks	Sale of the parks to the private sector	Tentatively scheduled for 2001
Financial sector		
Monetary and Financial Code	Strengthen central bank independence and banking supervision and regulation	Approved by congress in October 1999, but vetoed by the executive; revised draft to be resubmitted
Social Security	Substitute pay-as-you-go with individually capitalized system	Approved by congress in April 2001
Capital Markets Law	Establish policy and regulatory framework for capital market development	Approved by congress in May 2000. Establishment of administrative regulations pending
External sector		
General customs	Make customs system more efficient and transparent	Approved by senate in July 1998; not transmitted to the chamber of deputies
Tariff reform	Liberalize trade and reduce tariffs	Approved by congress in December 2000
Export incentive	Promote exports through system of drawbacks on custom duties and levies	Approved by congress in August 1999; administrative regulations approved in February 2000
Public sector reform		
Integrated Financial Management (IFM) system for public sector	Government to have full control over all resources—sources, uses, and accounting. Aim is to improve efficiency and transparency of government operations	IFM project approved by congress in October 2000
Modernization of the executive power	Improve macroeconomic policy coordination, streamline government structure	Congressional approval pending
Regulatory reform		
Property rights regulation	Establish new property rights law	Approved by congress in July 2000. Establishment of administrative regulations pending
Electricity Law	Establish modern regulatory framework and regulatory body	Approved in the first reading by senate in August 2000; final approval pending
Petroleum Products Law	Establish a fixed tax on domestic fuel consumption	Approved by congress in November 2000; administrative regulations approved in March 2001
Market Order Code	(1) Promote competition in domestic markets for goods and services; (2) establish antitrust and unfair competition measures; (3) protect consumer rights; (4) protect copyright; (5) regulate intellectual property rights; (6) establish a specialized institute	Bills (4) and (5) approved in March 2000 and the administrative regulations being prepared; other bills are awaiting congressional approval

Superintendency of Banks, the Central Bank of the Dominican Republic is working to strengthen domestic prudential norms and regulations, bringing them more in line with international standards and best practices. This will help foster a deep, sound, and resilient financial system.

Financial deepening is fundamental to promoting domestic saving and channeling it toward the most productive investments. To this end, the Monetary and Financial Code and the Capital Markets Law[21] would strengthen the institutional setting, promote competition, and enhance transparency in financial and securities markets. Additional stimulus to finan-cial deepening would come from reform of the social security system, which, besides improving the quality and effectiveness of social services, should aim to promote private sector involvement through the development of privately managed pension funds. In addition, more competitive markets are crucial to fostering economic growth and development. The Market Order Code[22] aims to remove impediments to competition in domestic markets for goods and services by establishing antitrust and unfair competition measures, protecting consumer rights, and regulating copyright and intellectual property rights.

[21]The Capital Markets Law was approved in May 2000, although the establishment of administrative regulations is still pending.

[22]Two of six bills associated with the Market Order Code were approved in March 2000, although as with the Capital Markets Law, the associated administrative regulations are still pending.

Appendix I   Governance Issues

Good governance is crucial to promoting economic stability, high-quality growth, and the implementation of second-generation reforms. It entails guaranteeing the rule of law, promoting the accountability, efficiency, and transparency of the public sector, and tackling corruption.

Several indicators capture the concept of governance in a country. According to the International Country Risk Guide, the government stability index in the Dominican Republic is 10 (the higher the value, the lower the risk), comparing favorably with the average of 9 for selected Latin American countries (LAC) (see Table 3).[23] The indices for corruption and law and order are both 4, above the LAC average of 3. Democratic accountability is 4, the same as the LAC average. Bureaucracy quality is 1, below the LAC average of 2. Total points for the five indices for the Dominican Republic come to 23, one point above the LAC average. Overall, these indices suggest that the Dominican Republic compares favorably with other LAC.

Public Fund Management

The Office of the Presidency, through Fund 14.01, is responsible for approximately 10 percent of central government spending (down from 50–60 percent several years ago). This fund lacks transparency and is highly discretional. In addition, budgeting, treasury, accounting, internal control, and government procurement systems are not well coordinated. Information is often exchanged manually or counted twice, and is frequently unreliable. These weaknesses hinder efficient resource allocation and provision of public services. To address these problems, the government, with technical assistance from the IDB, has approved an integrated financial management program, which will contribute to an efficient allocation and management of public funds and an increase

in transparency. The authorities intend to complete the program in 2002.

Modernization of the Executive Power

Efficient public administration is hampered by a lack of formal mechanisms for policy coordination, leading to overlapping responsibilities among public sector institutions. Other factors impeding efficient public administration include low-skilled labor, excess public sector employment, and weak information systems. In its efforts to reform, the government has requested assistance from the IDB to support modernizing the executive power by building institutional capacity, developing a more equitable distributional policy, and improving the efficiency of social spending. This reform is being considered by congress.

Anti-Corruption

Government restrictions can be sources of rent seeking and corruption. High tariffs, poorly targeted subsidies, price controls on agricultural products, and multiple currency practices in the Dominican Republic need to be reduced or eliminated. The government, aware of these problems, has enacted tariff and tax reforms, and is pursuing the privatization of state-owned enterprises, revising the monetary and financial code, improving property rights, and working on a modern regulatory framework for the electricity sector.

References

International Country Risk Guide, available on CD-ROM, by Political Risk Services Group (Syracuse, NY).

Kopits, George, and Jon Craig, 1998, *Transparency in Government Operations,* IMF Occasional Paper No. 158 (Washington: International Monetary Fund).

Leone, Alfredo Mario, 1997, "Stabilization, Structural Reforms and Challenges Ahead," IMF mimeo.

---

[23]The maximum assigned to government stability is 12 points, for corruption 6, law and order 6, democratic accountability 6, and bureaucracy quality 4.

Table 3. Selected Political Risk Components—Comparison with Western Hemisphere Countries[1,2]

(Average, 1997–99)

	Government Stability	Corruption	Law and Order	Democratic Accountability	Bureaucracy Quality	Total
Argentina	9	2	5	5	3	24
Bahamas	10	4	4	4	3	25
Bolivia	10	3	3	4	2	22
Brazil	10	3	2	4	2	21
Chile	10	4	5	4	3	26
Colombia	10	2	2	3	2	18
Costa Rica	10	5	4	5	2	26
Cuba	10	2	5	0	2	19
Dominican Republic	**10**	**4**	**4**	**4**	**1**	**23**
Ecuador	10	3	3	4	2	22
El Salvador	9	4	3	4	2	22
Guatemala	10	4	2	4	2	22
Guyana	9	3	4	5	3	24
Haiti	5	2	3	2	0	12
Honduras	10	2	2	4	2	20
Jamaica	10	3	3	5	3	24
Mexico	10	3	2	5	3	23
Nicaragua	10	4	4	6	1	25
Panama	9	2	3	6	3	23
Paraguay	8	2	4	4	1	18
Peru	9	3	3	2	2	19
Suriname	9	3	3	4	2	21
Trinidad and Tobago	10	3	4	5	3	25
Uruguay	10	3	3	5	2	23
Venezuela	9	3	4	5	1	22
Average	**9**	**3**	**3**	**4**	**2**	**22**

Source: International Country Risk Guide.

[1]The lower the risk point total, the higher the risk.

[2]The maximum assigned to government stability is 12 points, for corruption 6, law and order 6, democratic accountability 6, and bureaucracy quality 4.

II   Trade Reform Continues

During the early 1990s, the Dominican Republic undertook a number of important reforms to liberalize its trade regime. The most significant reforms took place in September 1990 as part of the New Economic Program, when the protectionist regime, which shielded domestic producers with high tariffs and cumbersome nontariff barriers, was largely dismantled. These reforms were consolidated in 1991–92, when the authorities simplified the exchange rate system and introduced a series of tax reforms that eliminated several important trade-based taxes, including all export taxes.

In tandem with these tax and tariff reforms, the Dominican Republic has also sought to improve trade relations with its neighbors through a series of multilateral and bilateral trade arrangements. This has included membership in the World Trade Organization (WTO), the Association of Caribbean States (ACS), CAFTA, CARICOM, and the concession of parity with the North American Free Trade Agreement (NAFTA) for access to the U.S. market.

This paper examines the trade reforms undertaken by the Dominican authorities during the 1990s. While the Dominican Republic has made significant progress toward liberalizing its trade and exchange system, further reform is necessary to harmonize its trade policies with those of its neighbors and to lower import tariff barriers. The openness of the trade regime is effectively increased by an extensive network of free-trade zones, but hampered by multiple currency practices, including a 5 percent foreign exchange commission.

The Trade Regime Prior to the 1990 Reforms

Like many countries in Latin America, the Dominican Republic had by the mid-1980s developed a restrictive trade system, with high import tariffs, a system of pervasive exemptions, prohibited export lists, export taxes, exchange restrictions, and multiple ex-change rate arrangements.[24] This system sought to develop import-substituting manufacturing industries. In addition, periodic balance of payments crises prompted the authorities to introduce further measures, which increased both the overall restrictiveness and the administrative complexity of the system.

Beyond creating vast economic inefficiencies, the system invited rent-seeking activities and, in some cases, outright corruption. The complexity of the system ensured that serious monitoring of customs administration was impossible. The array of exemptions and overvalued multiple exchange rates made misclassification and wrongful valuation of imports and exports commonplace. Groups or individuals with special interests pursued personal advantages arising from restrictive licensing and nontariff barriers.

The trade system also created a strong anti-export bias. This bias has most seriously affected traditional agriculture, where heavy export taxes were levied on sugar, bananas, coffee, and cocoa, and export receipts had to be surrendered at the official exchange rate. In addition, all exports were subject to a foreign exchange commission of 1½ percent of revenues. The tariff system was particularly restrictive and lacked transparency. It included both specific and ad valorem tariffs, which were cumulative. In some cases, nominal tariff rates in excess of 200 percent were imposed. This system was extremely complex to administer.

In line with the import-substituting objective, tariff exemptions also helped to greatly increase effective protection for domestic industries. Firms that were registered as import-substituting could obtain tariff exemptions for their imports of raw materials and intermediate inputs. Individual enterprises often obtained total or partial exemptions through special contracts with the government. The government also passed a series of laws and decrees which provided further specific exemptions on an ad hoc basis.

---

[24]The World Bank Country Study, *Dominican Republic: Economic Prospects and Policies to Renew Growth* (1985), provides an extensive survey of the trade regime and resulting impediments to economic growth.

Import prohibitions and other nontariff barriers were widespread. As part of a series of measures introduced to resolve the balance of payments crisis of 1979, the authorities introduced a list of prohibited imports covering more than 150 types of consumer goods such as certain garments, furniture, and light industrial goods. In 1982, the list was expanded to cover a further 200 items.

Throughout the 1980s, the central bank maintained a multiple currency system, with several overvalued official exchange rates.[25] Inevitably, a parallel exchange market emerged. These exchange arrangements heightened the anti-export bias, as manufacturing exporters were also required to surrender a proportion of their receipts at disadvantageous official rates. In contrast, importers of tariff-exempt goods could exchange domestic currency at advantageous overvalued rates.

The authorities made several attempts to unify the exchange rate. Unfortunately, these efforts were short-lived, as frequent balance of payments crises forced the authorities to use administrative measures to maintain the supply of foreign currency needed for official use. The exchange system became extremely restrictive after a crisis in June 1987, when the central bank requisitioned foreign exchange from all commercial banks, to become the sole provider of foreign exchange.

Trade Reforms in the 1990s

Poor export performance during the 1980s, coupled with persistent balance of payments problems, prompted the authorities to reevaluate their import-substituting development strategy. As part of the New Economic Program, the Dominican authorities undertook a wide-ranging reform of their trade system.[26] The tariff system was simplified by reducing the number of import taxes. Most import quotas, import licensing requirements, and import prohibitions were abolished. Agricultural export taxes were suspended. In an attempt to provide a more neutral tax regime, all tax incentives and ad hoc measures, except those specifically applying to the free-trade zones, were eliminated.

In January 1991, the authorities began the process of reforming the exchange system. While still for-

mally maintaining a dual exchange rate system, they introduced a freely determined interbank rate. In practice, the official rate is revalued fairly often and the spread between the official and interbank exchange rates has narrowed.[27] In 1993, the central bank started to reduce the number of export items that were subject to surrender requirements.

The initial trade liberalization was further consolidated during the tax reform of 1992. The import surcharge was reduced from 15 percent to 10 percent, and a program was announced for its eventual abolition by 1995. By 1993, most export restrictions, such as export licensing, minimum export prices for agricultural products, and all export taxes were abolished. Furthermore, the export administration system was greatly simplified when most special registration and documentation requirements were eliminated and only minor obligations kept for statistical purposes. Customs administration has benefited from the automation of customs documentation, which has reduced the discretion allowed to customs officers. However, the customs department maintains that significant undervaluation of imports remains a problem that it is determined to address by rigorously applying the law to value imports at their true commercial value, using updated valuation schedules.

The latest tariff reform, which came into effect in January 2001, has narrowed the tariff structure to five from nine non-zero rates and reduced the maximum from 35 percent to 20 percent, levied on all imports on an ad valorem basis (Table 4). As a result, the simple average tariff is estimated to have decreased to 10.7 percent from 17.7 percent. The most common rate was 10 percent for about 28 percent of all tariff lines; it is now 3 percent and 20 percent, each affecting 38 percent of all lines. A consumption tax (*Impuesto Selectivo al Consumo*) of between 5 percent and 80 percent levied at customs on certain luxury goods was also reduced to a range of 25 percent to 75 percent, applicable to a much smaller number of consumer goods, including passenger cars. This has brought the simple average tariff down to 11.4 percent, from 18.6 percent. Taxation is based upon the c.i.f. value and the amount of prior taxes and duties.

The current system maintains a number of import tariff exemptions. Most notably, products used in the agricultural sector, for example, insecticides, herbicides, and pesticides, remain exempt, as are certain goods regarded as socially critical, like medicines. A

---

[25]In addition to maintaining a multiple currency system, the Dominican Republic also maintained many other exchange restrictions, most notably a limitation on the level of permissible profit remittances.

[26]Initially, the tariff reform was conducted by means of presidential decrees (339–90 and 340–90). These decrees were subsequently ratified by congress in 1993 (Law No. 14–93).

---

[27]On various occasions the spread between the official and interbank rate has become substantial. Under the draft Monetary and Financial Code, under consideration in congress, the exchange rates would be fully unified through the elimination of all surrender requirements.

Table 4. Import Tariff Structure[1]
(Excluding selective consumption tax)

Pre-2001 Import Tariff Schedule			2001 Import Tariff Reform		
Tariff Bands (percent)	Number of Lines	In Percent of Total Lines	Tariff Bands (percent)	Number of Lines	In Percent of Total Lines
0.0	8	0	0.0	353	6
1.5	19	0	1.5	19	0
3.0	345	6	3.0	2,397	38
5.0	648	10	8.0	561	9
10.0	1,749	28	14.0	586	9
15.0	561	9	20.0	2,355	38
20.0	586	9			
25.0	827	13			
30.0	970	15			
35.0	558	9			
Total	**6,271**	**100**	**Total**	**6,271**	**100**
Memorandum item:					
Simple average import tariff		17.7			10.7
Simple average import tariff[2]		18.6			11.4

Sources: Dominican authorities; and IMF staff estimates.

[1]Does not include contingent tariffs that may be applied to beans, chicken, garlic, milk, onions, rice, corn, and sugar.

[2]Including selective consumption tax on imports.

number of export prohibitions are also maintained to supply the domestic food market. Exports of unprocessed wood, charcoal, and certain animal species are forbidden on environmental grounds.

The tariff system still offers important effective tariff protection to many domestically produced goods. According to the WTO, significant tariff escalation exists, especially for the more processed products. The WTO argues that tariff escalation is particularly pronounced for textiles and leather products.

While the majority of formal nontariff barriers were abolished, certain quotas were maintained on eight important basic consumption goods—beans, chicken, corn, garlic, milk, onions, rice, and sugar. During the Uruguay Round of multilateral trade negotiations, the Dominican Republic agreed to eliminate all nontariff barriers and introduce a maximum tariff bound of 40 percent. However, it also sought a waiver on its WTO obligations with respect to these eight products, which allows it to introduce tariff rates above the agreed bounds and maintain nontariff quotas. The issue remained unresolved during the Uruguay Round. In early 1999, the WTO accepted the Dominican authorities' proposal to amend their WTO schedule of concessions (through the procedures outlined in Article XVIII of the WTO Agreement). This permits the Dominican Republic to set a two-tier tariff structure for each of the eight prod-

ucts. The authorities may charge tariffs, ranging from 5 percent to 25 percent on imports below a specified import volume, while maintaining a maximum tariff bound of 40 percent. Imports in excess of the specified limits (Table 5) could be subjected to higher tariff rates, known as contingent tariffs, ranging from 60 percent to 137 percent in 1999 (Table 6). The authorities have also announced a schedule under which these contingent tariffs will be reduced to between 40 percent and 99 percent by 2005.

In March 1998, a number of nontariff barriers, which had been created by either presidential or administrative decree, were abolished. While many formal nontariff barriers have been abolished, importers may still face serious administrative trade barriers. For example, in a backlash against alleged pervasive undervaluation of imports, some importers complain that customs valuations are discretionary, while arbitrary customs clearance procedures can delay the importation of merchandise, according to the U.S. Department of Commerce. Import permits that are required for certain agricultural items are also sometimes delayed or withheld.

The Dominican Republic still maintains surrender requirements for selected exports of goods and services. Foreign exchange proceeds from traditional agricultural products have to be surrendered in full to the central bank at the official exchange rate, as must

Table 5. Initial Import Level Before Contingent Tariff Applies
(In metric tons)

Product	1999	2000	2001	2002	2003	2004	2005
Rice	11,898	12,410	12,943	13,450	14,028	14,632	15,261
Garlic	3,600	3,750	3,900	4,050	4,200	4,350	4,500
Sugar	24,000	25,000	26,000	27,000	28,000	29,000	30,000
Chicken	8,500	9,000	9,500	10,000	10,500	11,000	11,500
Onions	3,000	3,125	3,250	3,375	3,500	3,625	3,750
Beans	14,400	15,000	15,600	16,200	16,800	17,400	18,000
Milk	32,000	32,000	32,000	32,000	32,000	32,000	32,000
Corn	858,200	897,000	935,800	974,600	1,013,400	1,052,200	1,091,000

Source: Dominican authorities.

Table 6. Schedule of Contingent Tariffs[1]
(In percent)

Product	Basic Tariff	1999	2000	2001	2002	2003	2004	2005
Rice	20	114	111.5	109	106.5	104	101.5	99
Garlic	25	111	109	107	105	103	101	99
Sugar	20	94	93	91	90	88	87	85
Chicken	25	137	131	124	118	112	105	99
Onions	25	97	97	97	97	97	97	97
Beans	25	95	94	93	92	91	90	89
Milk	20	84	79	74	70	65	60	56
Corn	5	60	57	54	50	47	43	40

Source: Dominican authorities.
[1] Tariffs only apply when imports exceed a pre-specified amount, as specified in Table 5 above.

those from certain services such as telecommunications, credit card transactions, and remittances from insurance claims. Passage of a new Monetary and Financial Code would abolish these discriminatory obligations.

Despite significant progress made during the early 1990s, and with the new import tariff rates in effect, the Dominican Republic maintains a trade regime that is still more restrictive than those of its major regional neighbors, as measured by the IMF's Trade Restrictiveness Index[28] (Table 7). The Dominican

[28] For further information on the construction of this index, see *Trade Liberalization in IMF-supported Programs* (1998). This index should be interpreted carefully in the case of the Dominican Republic because it only refers to tariffs paid on imports to the domestic economy; it excludes the tariff system that applies to imports into the free-trade zones.

Republic also has higher import tariff rates on a simple average than these countries, but trade dispersion is relatively low (Table 8).

Following up on the reduction of import tariffs at the beginning of 2001, further legislation is pending to initiate the second stage of trade liberalization. This would reduce the number of tariff rates to four, while the new maximum rate would be 15 percent. More specifically, the tariff structure would be as follows: a zero tariff rate for raw materials not produced domestically and all capital goods, 5 percent for domestically produced raw materials and intermediate goods not produced domestically, 10 percent for domestically produced intermediate goods, and 15 percent for final consumption goods.

The diffuse nature of trade policymaking is regarded as a major weakness of the trade regime,

Table 7. Index of Trade Restrictiveness
Selected Caribbean and Central American
Countries, as of end-2000

	Tariff Barriers	Nontariff Barriers	Overall Trade Restrictiveness
Belize	2	2	5
Costa Rica	1	2	4
El Salvador	1	2	4
Guatemala	1	2	4
Haiti	1	1	1
Honduras	1	1	1
Jamaica	1	2	4
Trinidad and Tobago	1	2	4
Dominican Republic[1]	**2**	**2**	**5**

Sources: Dominican authorities; and IMF staff estimates.
[1]As per 2001, taking into account the reformed tariff structure.

tending to slow the pace of trade reform.[29] While the Ministry of Industry and Trade determines trade policy, the Ministry of Foreign Affairs has the responsibility for negotiating and concluding international treaties and agreements. However, the National Sugar Institute has direct responsibility for all issues relating to sugar, including trade, while the Ministry

—————
[29]WTO, *Trade Policy Review*, 1996.

of Agriculture has various technical responsibilities related to the management of the agricultural trade regime. Matters are further complicated by the existence of a number of special commissions and interministerial committees in charge of coordinating, of reforming trade policy, or of regulating certain sector activities—for example, the Foreign Trade Commission, the National Free-Trade Zones Council, the National Council for Development, and the Tariff Study Commission.

The authorities have tried to resolve coordination difficulties with respect to new trade agreements. In line with a WTO recommendation, the National Trade Negotiation Commission was created in 1997. It has ultimate responsibility for negotiating all new trade arrangements. However, technical discussions still remain the responsibility of the relevant ministry or government body. At various times, the authorities have also considered creating a new ministry that would be responsible for all trade policy issues.

Free-Trade Zones

Over the last 30 years, the Dominican Republic has developed an extensive system of industrial free-trade zones (FTZ). Their rapid growth in terms of employment, export value, and the number of firms has been remarkable. In 2000, there were 46 industrial parks, containing around 500 enterprises, employing almost 200,000 employees inside the FTZ (8 percent of total employment), and providing possibly twice as many jobs outside the FTZ. The FTZ attract-

Table 8. Import Tariff Rates
Selected Caribbean and Central American Countries, as of end-2000

	Simple Average	Minimum	Maximum	Trade Weighted Average	Standard Deviation	Description of Bands
Belize	9.2	...	25.0	8.6	13.3	...
Costa Rica	7.2	...	253.0	...	13.8	...
El Salvador	5.6	...	40.0	8.5	7.9	12 bands
Guatemala	7.3	...	27.0	...	8.1	4 bands of 1, 9, 14, and 19 percent
Haiti	9.0	...	15.0	...	...	4 bands of 0, 5, 10, and 15 percent
Honduras	7.8	1.0	55.0	...	8.0	13 bands
Jamaica	8.9	0	75.0	...	12.4	...
Trinidad and Tobago	9.1	0	45.0	16.7	11.6	10 bands
Dominican Republic[1,2]	**10.7**	**0.0**	**20.0**	**...**	**7.4**	**6 bands ranging from 0 to 20 percent**

Sources: Dominican authorities; and IMF staff estimates.
[1]As per 2001, taking into account the reformed tariff structure.
[2]Does not include the selective consumption tax or the contingent tariffs applied to beans, chicken, garlic, milk, onions, rice, corn, and sugar.

ed important amounts of foreign direct investment and generated gross exports of an estimated US$4.8 billion, accounting for 83 percent of total exports; net export receipts were US$1.7 billion. Since 1994, net FTZ export receipts (in U.S. dollar terms) have grown, on average, by 15 percent a year (Table 9). Local expenditure of enterprises in the FTZ in 2000 has been estimated at US$1 billion.

The FTZ's rapid growth can be explained by three main factors. First, the regulations governing operation and activity are generally regarded by both domestic and foreign investors as stable and transparent, in contrast to the legal framework applying to "domestic" exports.[30] Second, the tax incentives offered to enterprises located in FTZ are considered attractive.[31] Finally, the advantage of close location to the United States and Puerto Rico, coupled with participation in several preferential regional trade arrange-

ments, has facilitated growth. These arrangements allowed the Dominican Republic to strengthen the competitive advantage of its FTZ through regulated market access, but resulted in a strong orientation of FTZ exports toward the U.S. market and hence a potentially heavy dependence on the U.S. business cycle. However, this is partially compensated by other sources of foreign exchange, such as tourism, which are derived mainly from Europe.

Trade Agreements

As part of the outward reorientation of trade policy, the Dominican Republic has actively promoted closer formal trading relations in the region and with

[30]FTZ are considered extraterritorial with respect to the Dominican economy, but they can trade with the "domestic" economy, subject to applicable tariffs and regulations.

[31]Enterprises locating to FTZ are exempt from corporate income tax, construction taxes, fees relating to the registration of

loan agreements, charges related to transfers of real estate, and VAT. Furthermore, they are exempt from standard import duties, including duties on materials and equipment used in the establishment and operation of the company. For a full description of the tax incentives offered to enterprises locating in free-trade zones, see *Legal Guide to the Free Zones of the Dominican Republic* (Pellerano and Herrera, 1999).

Table 9. Free-Trade Zone Activity

	Number of Firms (Units)	Number of Employees (Thousands)	Foreign Exchange Generated[1]	Gross Value of Exports	Textile Exports of Which
			(In millions of U.S. dollars)		
1980	71	16.4	45	276	...
1981	77	18.3	58	358	...
1982	87	18.7	61	379	...
1983	101	19.3	62	384	...
1984	120	25.7	52	323	...
1985	136	30.9	45	277	...
1986	156	51.2	89	549	...
1987	199	66.0	98	609	...
1988	220	83.8	130	807	...
1989	299	122.9	191	1187	...
1990	331	130.0	196	850	...
1991	366	135.3	250	1053	...
1992	404	141.1	306	1195	...
1993	462	164.3	401	2609	1,458
1994	467	176.3	441	2716	1,616
1995	469	165.6	512	2907	1,787
1996	436	164.3	545	3107	1,802
1997	446	182.2	698	3596	2,273
1998	496	196.0	827	4100	2,395
1999	473	191.1	887	4332	2,385
2000	491	206.3	1,018	4771	2,571

Sources: ONAPLAN; National Council of Exports Free-Trade Zone; and BCRD.

[1]On March 20, 1992, surrender requirements for FTZ foreign exchange earnings were abolished. Thereafter, foreign exchange generated is an estimation of local expenditures of FTZ enterprises.

the rest of the world. Its accession in March 1995 to WTO membership provided a particularly strong incentive to accelerate trade liberalization and pass new legislation to comply with the organization's requirements. These included legislation on foreign investment and telecommunications, which provided a boost to these activities.

During the 1990s, the Dominican Republic joined a number of regional organizations and it participates in the Free Trade Area of the Americas (FTAA). It was a founding member of the Association of Caribbean States (ACS), a body launched in January 1995. The ACS promotes trade liberalization and regional economic integration within the Caribbean basin. The Dominican Republic has observer status with the CARICOM, which aims to deepen economic integration among its member countries through establishing a common market, coordinating and regulating commercial and economic relations, and defining a common position in other regional trade initiatives, such as the FTAA. In February 2001, congress ratified a trade agreement with CARICOM (excluding Haiti, which joined CARICOM after trade negotiations between the Dominican Republic and CARICOM members had begun). In 1999, the Dominican Republic joined the CAFTA, which aims to deepen and diversify trade relations among its member countries; an agreement with its members has just received congressional approval.

The Dominican Republic enjoys important preferential access to the U.S. market. The Caribbean Basin Initiative, which was introduced in 1984 to promote trade relations and foreign investment between the Caribbean and the United States, provides duty-free access for most products, except petroleum, footwear, canned tuna, and certain watches. Since 2000, the United States has provided free access for Dominican textile products with minimal or no U.S. components, provided they do not contain any third-country components. This will allow the Dominican textile industry to diversify further within the sector through increased production of intermediate goods and raw materials and to integrate vertically, adding cutting, weaving, and spinning to its production process. General quotas are maintained for access to the U.S. market of certain textile products, but the arrangement allows for yearly negotiations among competing Caribbean partner countries to determine their respective market shares. New WTO rulings establish, however, that all quotas be phased out by the end of 2004, challenging Dominican textile exporters to compete in a deregulated environment and the country to diversify its export base even more.

The Dominican Republic benefits from preferred access to U.S. markets through the generalized system of preferences, which gives duty-free access to a wide range of products, and to the European Union through the Lomé Convention and its successor agreements. In October 2000, the Dominican Republic was granted parity with NAFTA members Canada and Mexico for access to U.S. markets, with respect to all goods. This is expected to give another boost to textile exports in particular, which face strong competition from Mexico. However, negotiations between the United States and other countries for NAFTA parity may over time reduce the benefits of this advantage for the Dominican Republic. Not being an initial signatory to the EU's Lomé Convention, and in order to gain membership in the group of African, Caribbean, and Pacific countries (ACP), the Dominican Republic had to unilaterally revoke certain preferential provisions of the convention relating to export products such as sugar, bananas, and rum.[32]

Conclusion

During the early 1990s, the Dominican Republic made significant progress in liberalizing its trade system. Much of the old system, which aimed at fostering domestic import-substituting industries, has now been dismantled. Most important, tariff rates have been simplified and reduced, most nontariff barriers have been eliminated, and export taxes have been abolished. Much of the administrative complexity that characterized the old system has disappeared. There is still some unfinished business, however, as some restrictive and interventionist elements of the pre-1990 system have survived.

Gradual trade liberalization with respect to the domestic economy, comprising agriculture, mining, and nontradable goods, and a completely free trade and tax regime favoring the emergence of high-growth, outward-oriented industrial production in free-trade zones and tourism has resulted in a dualistic economic structure. In order to address these differences, which are also reflected in growing regional and social differences, and to generalize the efficient use of resources, the Dominican authorities intend to conclude their tariff reform by further reducing tariff levels and dispersion, to streamline administrative procedures, and to reduce the foreign exchange commission. Approval of a new Monetary and Financial Code, which has been with the congress for quite some time, would eliminate persisting multiple currencies practices by abolishing remaining foreign exchange surrender requirements and unifying the exchange rate, two other objectives of the current government and indispensable elements

---

[32]For further details on trade relations between the Dominican Republic and the European Union, see *Libro Verde sobre las Relaciones Entre la Unión Europea y los países ACP en los albores del siglo XXI* (European Commission, 1996).

for establishing a consistent and efficient trade and foreign exchange regime.

References

Consejo Nacional de Zonas Francas de Exportación, various issues, *Informe estadístico del sector Zonas Francas* (Santo Domingo).

European Commission, 1996, *Libro Verde sobre las Relaciones Entre la Unión Europea y los países ACP en los albores del siglo XXI* (Luxembourg: Official Publications Office of the European Communities).

International Monetary Fund, 1998, *Trade Liberalization in IMF-Supported Programs* (Washington: International Monetary Fund).

Pellerano and Herrera, 1999, *Legal Guide to the Free Zones of the Dominican Republic,* State Secretariat of Industry and Commerce (Santo Domingo).

United States Department of Commerce, 1999, "Dominican Republic: Foreign Trade Barriers," *National trade estimate report on foreign trade barriers* (Washington).

World Bank, 1985, *Dominican Republic: Economic Prospects and Policies to Renew Growth* (Washington: World Bank Group).

World Trade Organization, 1996, *Dominican Republic: Trade Policy Review* (Geneva).

III   Successful External Debt Restructuring

In the 1960s and early 1970s the Dominican Republic enjoyed sustained economic growth together with relatively low inflation. In the late 1970s, however, the country began to experience severe external and internal imbalances. High fuel import prices and international interest rates, the precipitous fall in non-oil commodity prices, and a world recession led to a record external current account deficit of 10 percent of GDP in 1980. The authorities resorted to external arrears accumulation as a means of financing this deficit. At the end of 1980, arrears on commercial transactions amounted to about US$150 million; by 1982 the amount in arrears had jumped to US$436 million and included not only commercial arrears, but also debt-service payments and profit remittances.

The 1980s—First Round of External Debt Restructuring

In 1983, following the formalization of a Stand-By Arrangement supported by the IMF, the Dominican authorities initiated a round of discussions with commercial banks to restructure principal in arrears and unpaid letters of credit. Unfortunately, the restructuring in December of that same year only provided temporary relief to the country's balance of payments problems, and by the end of 1984, the Dominican authorities had to initiate a new round of negotiations with commercial banks.[33] In February 1986, a new rescheduling agreement was signed with international commercial banks for US$775 million, including previously rescheduled debt, arrears up to the end of 1985, and public debt maturing before the end of 1989. In May 1985, the Dominican authorities agreed with Paris Club creditors to reschedule US$290 million. However, due to a lack of international reserves, the high level of outstanding debt, and the unwillingness of the national congress to approve some of the clauses, the Dominican Republic

was unable to comply with the agreement. Efforts to reach a new agreement in 1987 failed in the absence of an IMF-supported program, a prerequisite to concluding an agreement with the Paris Club.

The government that took office in 1986 embarked on an economic reactivation program and, lacking external financing, it resorted to loose fiscal and monetary policies. The success of the program was short-lived—by 1989 average inflation had increased to 41 percent (from 5 percent in 1986), the peso was devalued on several occasions, and the external current account deficits were once again being financed by a running down of international reserves and the accumulation of external arrears.

The 1990s—Second Round of External Debt Restructuring

After being reelected in May 1990, President Balaguer introduced a series of measures aimed at reducing the fiscal deficit. This effort eventually led to the conclusion of a Stand-By Arrangement with the IMF in 1991. At that time, Latin America was receiving massive net capital inflows and international creditors were generally supportive of countries' efforts to reform their economies. This allowed the Dominican Republic to benefit in the first half of the 1990s from substantial debt relief from bilateral creditors and commercial banks. This contributed to an easing of the country's external public sector debt-service burden and facilitated macroeconomic adjustment. By the end of 1999, the public sector's total debt was brought down to a manageable 21 percent of GDP, from 72 percent of GDP at the end of 1990 (Table 10). Similarly, annual debt service due was reduced from 13 percent of GDP in 1990 to 2 percent of GDP in 1999 (Table 11). Outstanding arrears were eliminated by the end of 1998, compared with almost US$1.5 billion (23 percent of GDP) at the end of 1990 (Table 12). The debt relief agreements also provided a means for the Dominican authorities to reestablish normal relations with most external creditors, a primary goal of the authorities' economic program.

---

[33]The Dominican Republic experienced another adverse external shock in 1984–85. World sugar prices dropped sharply and import quotas to the United States were reduced substantially. International real interest rates remained high and external financing dried up.

Table 10. Outstanding External Public Sector Debt (End-of-Period)

	1990	1991	1992	1993	1994	1995	1996	1997	1998	1999
	(In millions of U.S. dollars)									
Total	**4,499**	**4,614**	**4,413**	**4,562**	**3,946**	**3,999**	**3,807**	**3,572**	**3,545**	**3,657**
Multilateral	**1,080**	**1,096**	**1,106**	**1,172**	**1,228**	**1,293**	**1,194**	**1,071**	**1,137**	**1,236**
IDB	700	695	668	673	708	798	802	784	820	850
World Bank	246	254	261	259	279	282	244	208	204	275
IMF	74	20	19	19	18	17	17	16	15	15
OPEC	22	89	123	186	190	160	96	29	56	54
Other	38	38	35	35	34	35	36	35	42	42
Bilateral	**2,301**	**2,288**	**2,019**	**2,012**	**1,927**	**1,874**	**1,793**	**1,695**	**1,718**	**1,754**
Paris Club	1,664	1,779	1,760	1,732	1,705	1,670	1,607	1,519	1,564	1,586
France	26	31	31	33	43	54	49	43	44	38
Germany	89	92	88	75	78	82	74	62	80	74
Italy	44	63	58	61	60	59	58	55	54	51
Japan	230	265	249	245	253	235	197	161	179	198
Spain	300	321	329	301	286	279	282	289	319	380
United States	973	1,003	1,003	1,015	980	956	944	907	886	844
Other Paris Club	3	4	3	3	4	4	3	2	2	2
Other bilateral	637	509	259	280	222	204	186	176	154	168
Argentina	36	30	30	24	0	0	0	0	0	0
Brazil	20	11	11	0	0	0	0	0	7	32
Colombia	30	18	18	17	13	10	7	5	2	0
Mexico	139	0	0	26	0	0	0	0	0	0
Peru	8	9	9	6	6	6	6	6	6	6
Taiwan Province of China	6	7	7	8	8	9	0	0	0	0
Venezuela	392	434	182	198	194	179	173	165	138	130
Other	5	0	0	0	0	0	0	0	0	0
Commercial banks	**971**	**1,074**	**1,134**	**1,261**	**613**	**662**	**651**	**687**	**604**	**619**
Suppliers and others	**147**	**157**	**154**	**116**	**178**	**170**	**169**	**120**	**87**	**48**
	(In percent of GDP)									
Total	**71.9**	**60.4**	**49.1**	**46.8**	**36.6**	**33.0**	**28.1**	**23.5**	**22.1**	**20.9**
Multilateral	17.3	14.3	12.3	12.0	11.4	10.7	8.8	7.1	7.1	7.1
Bilateral	36.8	30.0	22.5	20.6	17.9	15.5	13.2	11.2	10.7	10.0
Paris Club	26.6	23.3	19.6	17.8	15.8	13.8	11.8	10.0	9.8	9.1
Other bilateral	10.2	6.7	2.9	2.9	2.1	1.7	1.4	1.2	1.0	1.0
Commercial banks	15.5	14.1	12.6	12.9	5.7	5.5	4.8	4.5	3.8	3.5
Suppliers and others	2.3	2.0	1.7	1.2	1.6	1.4	1.2	0.8	0.5	0.3
	(In percent of total debt)									
Total	**100.0**	**100.0**	**100.0**	**100.0**	**100.0**	**100.0**	**100.0**	**100.0**	**100.0**	**100.0**
Multilateral	24.0	23.7	25.1	25.7	31.1	32.3	31.4	30.0	32.1	33.8
Bilateral	51.1	49.6	45.7	44.1	48.8	46.9	47.1	47.4	48.4	48.0
Paris Club	37.0	38.6	39.9	38.0	43.2	41.8	42.2	42.5	44.1	43.4
Other bilateral	14.2	11.0	5.9	6.1	5.6	5.1	4.9	4.9	4.3	4.6
Commercial banks	21.6	23.3	25.7	27.6	15.5	16.5	17.1	19.2	17.0	16.9
Suppliers and others	3.3	3.4	3.5	2.5	4.5	4.3	4.4	3.4	2.4	1.3
	(In millions of U.S. dollars, unless otherwise indicated)									
Memorandum items										
Total official debt	3,381	3,384	3,125	3,184	3,155	3,167	2,987	2,766	2,854	2,990
(in percent of total debt)	75.2	73.3	70.8	69.8	80.0	79.2	78.5	77	81	82
Total private debt	1,118	1,230	1,288	1,377	791	832	820	806	691	667
GDP[1]	6,259	7,637	8,988	9,750	10,785	12,102	13,560	15,171	16,030	17,476

Sources: BCRD; and IMF staff estimates.

[1] Derived using a weighted average exchange rate of the official and market exchange rates based on current account receipts.

Table 11. Medium- and Long-Term Public External Debt Service

	1990	1991	1992	1993	1994	1995	1996	1997	1998	1999
					(In millions of U.S. dollars)					
Total	**801**	**601**	**496**	**942**	**492**	**483**	**468**	**445**	**437**	**405**
Scheduled amortization	**490**	**306**	**250**	**674**	**301**	**253**	**251**	**256**	**250**	**225**
Of which: IMF repurchases	58	45	15	10	8	34	60	62	29	0
Paid	...	...	...	155	202	231	221	233	195	166
Rescheduled	...	...	...	24	61	0	14	10	18	6
Forgiven	...	...	...	0	0	0	0	0	0	0
New arrears[1]				495	38	22	16	14	37	52
Payment of arrears				30	75	27	16	22	14	46
Scheduled interest	**311**	**295**	**246**	**267**	**191**	**230**	**218**	**189**	**187**	**180**
Of which: on reserve liabilities	...	...	...	10	14	19	16	11	9	9
Of which: on arrears	85	115	99	78	67	15	16	12	2	0
Paid	...	...	...	143	124	143	121	114	111	97
Rescheduled	...	...	...	7	25	0	7	15	4	9
Forgiven	...	...	...	1	1	1	1	1	1	1
New arrears[1]				116	36	50	55	24	36	41
					(In percent of GDP)					
Total scheduled debt service	**12.8**	**7.9**	**5.5**	**9.7**	**4.6**	**4.0**	**3.5**	**2.9**	**2.7**	**2.3**
Amortization	7.8	4.0	2.8	6.9	2.8	2.1	1.8	1.7	1.6	1.3
Interest	5.0	3.9	2.7	2.7	1.8	1.9	1.6	1.2	1.2	1.0
Total paid debt service	**...**	**...**	**...**	**3.4**	**3.7**	**3.3**	**2.6**	**2.4**	**2.0**	**1.8**
Amortization	...	...	...	1.9	2.6	2.1	1.7	1.7	1.3	1.2
Interest	...	...	...	1.5	1.2	1.2	0.9	0.8	0.7	0.6

Sources: BCRD; and IMF staff estimates.
[1]In 1998/99, including informally agreed delay of debt service to Paris Club creditors.

Table 12. Outstanding External Public Sector Arrears (End-of-Period)[1]

	1990	1991	1992	1993	1994	1995	1996	1997	1998	1999
					(In millions of U.S. dollars)					
Total	**1,456**	**779**	**627**	**1,259**	**226**	**247**	**261**	**63**	**28**	**18**
Multilateral	**47**	**20**	**20**	**20**	**20**	**10**	**10**	**10**	**10**	**0**
Of which										
On IMF credits	27	...	...	...	...	...	...	...	...	...
Bilateral	**952**	**169**	**10**	**120**	**113**	**138**	**150**	**39**	**3**	**3**
Paris Club	734	...	...	75	85	118	149	25	2	2
Other bilateral	218	169	10	46	29	21	0	15	1	1
Commercial banks	**232**	**360**	**469**	**1,049**	**4**	**0**	**0**	**1**	**1**	**1**
Suppliers and others	**225**	**230**	**129**	**70**	**89**	**99**	**102**	**13**	**14**	**14**
Of which										
On reserve liabilities[2]	178	171	60	26	1	0	0	0	0	0
					(In percent of GDP)					
Total	23.3	10.2	7.0	12.9	2.1	2.0	1.9	0.4	0.2	0.1

Sources: BCRD; and IMF staff estimates.
[1]Includes past-due payments that are still within the grace period and debt service in dispute. Figures for 1998 and 1999 do not include arrears tolerated by Paris Club members as part of the relief following Hurricane Georges. As of June 30, 2000, all such arrears were cleared. As of December 1997, all outstanding arrears were regularized or cleared.
[2]On reserve liabilities other than IMF credits; some of the liabilities are due to official bilateral creditors.

In late 1991, the authorities were granted a rescheduling by Paris Club members and soon thereafter debt reduction packages were also concluded with Venezuela and Mexico, the two largest non-Paris Club bilateral creditors. A restructuring of debt with commercial banks, which included debt stock reductions, was agreed in early 1994 and implemented in August of that year. Each of these agreements also involved commitments to regularize relations with creditors, including a mix of cash payments and capitalization of arrears. In 1995, arrears were also cleared with Paraguay and Venezuela and, in 1997, with the U.S. Commodity Credit Corporation (CCC).

While the burden of outstanding external obligations was being reduced, the Dominican Republic's access to new loans remained limited. Following the restructuring of commercial bank debt in 1994, there were net capital outflows (except for a marginal reversal in 1995). Overall, the stock of external public debt fell from US$4.5 billion at the end of 1990 to US$3.7 billion at the end of 1999. While the stock of external debt owed to multilateral organizations increased by US$156 million, debt to bilateral creditors fell by US$547 million, and to commercial banks by US$352 million. In terms of debt composition, the share of outstanding external debt owed to official bilateral and multilateral creditors rose to 82 percent at the end of 1999 from 75 percent at the end of 1990. On the other hand, the share of commercial bank debt fell to 17 percent at the end of 1999, from 22 percent at the end of 1990 (see Figure 2). The change in composition of debt and the lack of fresh funds from commercial creditors reflect the weak credit rating of the government, which effectively impeded financial market access at acceptable terms.

After reaching a low in 1998, the stock of debt (in U.S. dollar terms) has edged up (while continuing to decrease in relation to GDP), as multilateral and bilateral lending picked up again. Over the years, as the external debt burden was declining, some deficiencies in the control and monitoring of public external borrowing built up. However, excessive recourse to external debt was avoided due to congressional unwillingness to approve more external loans, partly motivated by the experience with external overindebtedness in the 1980s. Nevertheless, in the run-up to the 2000 presidential elections, this political control of external debt contraction did not prevent the use of relatively expensive bilateral credits tied to specific investment projects. This shortened the average maturity and, together with a rise in repayments on some categories of rescheduled debt, led to a more uneven debt-service profile for 2000–01.

The remainder of this section describes the major debt relief packages. It then reviews the overall impact of the debt relief on annual debt-service obliga-

Figure 2. Changes in Composition of External Public Sector Debt
(In percent of total)

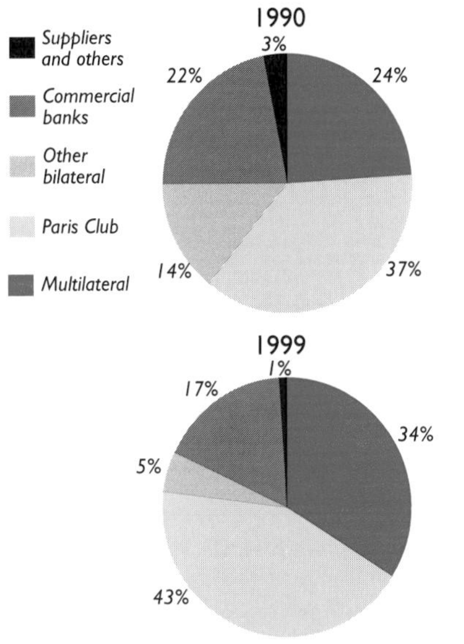

Sources: BCRD; and IMF staff estimates.

tions, including payments in arrears, future debt-service payments, and the composition of external debt, concluding with an outlook for external debt policy.

The 1991 Paris Club Debt Rescheduling

On November 22, 1991, the Dominican Republic agreed with its Paris Club creditors[34] on rescheduling obligations amounting to US$927 million (Table 13), of which US$144 million was interest on arrears outstanding at the beginning of the consolidation period. The authorities cleared US$113 million of arrears on debt ineligible for rescheduling, which was paid in early 1992. The agreement provided for repayment over 14 years, with an 8-year grace period. For concessional obligations, the repayment period was extended to 20 years with a 10-year grace period; for past-due interest, the repayment period was 10 years with a 5-year grace period. As a lower-middle-income country, the Dominican Republic

---

[34]Five member countries (France, Germany, Japan, Spain, and the United States) reached accords with the Dominican Republic.

Table 13. Total Rescheduled Debt

	Face Value of Rescheduling (In millions of U.S. dollars)	Terms	Special Features
1991 Paris Club debt repayment	927	Repayment of 14 years with 8-year grace period for nonconcessional debt. Repayment of 20 years with 10-year grace period for concessional debt. Repayment of 10 years with 5-year grace period for interest on arrears.	$113 million of arrears were paid in cash in 1992. Arrears with the IMF equivalent to $27 million also cleared.
1994 Commercial bank restructuring	1,251	35 percent of outstanding debt bought back at a 75 percent discount. Remaining principal exchanged for collateralized 30-year Brady Bonds. One-third of past-due interest (PDI) bought back at 75 percent discount. Remaining PDI bonds to be repaid within 15 years with 2.5-year grace period.	Total cash outlay of $169 million for debt buyback and interest payment in arrears. In addition, $39 million used to purchase collateral (30-year zero-coupon bonds). Total discount granted was $585 million.
1991–98 Non-Paris Club rescheduling	600	$425 million outstanding debt payments bought back at a 67 percent discount. $137 million to be repaid over 5 years with no grace period, with stepped up payments starting in 2001.	

Source: BCRD.

was not eligible for cancellation of any debt obligations. These terms were somewhat softer than those of the Dominican Republic's May 1985 agreement with the Paris Club, which allowed for a repayment period of only 9½ years and 5 years' grace.

Eligibility for rescheduling was partly established at the time of the 1985 Paris Club agreement. Only amortization, interest, and interest on arrears incurred prior to the cutoff date of June 30, 1984, were eligible for the 1991 rescheduling. Previously rescheduled debt service was also eligible for that rescheduling. An 18-month consolidation period (October 1, 1991 to March 31, 1993) was established, during which time current debt service falling due on pre-cutoff-date debt was also rescheduled. Many of the arrears outstanding at the beginning of the consolidation period were also rescheduled, including about US$300 million of arrears on previously rescheduled debt. The agreement also called for the successful completion of a program with the IMF over the consolidation

period, implying the clearance of US$27 million in arrears to the IMF.

Non-Paris Club Debt Rescheduling: 1991–97

The Paris Club urged the Dominican Republic to seek equivalent debt relief from non-Paris Club creditors to assure equitable burden-sharing. Mexico and Venezuela, the two largest non-Paris Club creditors to have provided project loans, balance of payments support, credits for petroleum imports, and export credits, granted generous restructuring terms. The Dominican Republic was given the opportunity to buy back much of the outstanding obligations at about one-third of their face value. Toward the end of 1991, US$160 million of debt outstanding to Mexico was repurchased for about US$50 million. After repeated prior reschedulings, about two-thirds of the US$265 million owed to Venezuela as of the end of 1991 was repurchased at a similar discount in March 1992. These two transactions reduced the Dominican Republic's debt by US$425 million at a cost of US$140 million. Arrears to Brazil and Peru were cleared in 1993 and arrears to Paraguay and Venezuela during 1995. Outstanding obligations to Taiwan Province of China, totaling about US$9 million, were rescheduled for repayment over the period 1996–98; penalty interest on these arrears was forgiven.

Though not technically a rescheduling, about US$20 million of overdue payments to the OPEC Fund, the development lending arm of the Organization of Petroleum Exporting Countries (OPEC), were also cleared in 1995 and 1996 through new credits for the exclusive use of repaying these arrears. Finally, in 1997, the Dominican Republic reached an agreement with the CCC. Under the new agreement, debt-service payments resumed and past-due interest and principal in the amount of US$137 million were made current. In contrast to reschedulings with other creditors, there

was no grace period and repayment was to occur over five years, with stepped up payments to start in June 2001, at a fixed interest rate of 6½ percent.

The 1994 Restructuring of Commercial Bank Credits

After prolonged negotiations with the commercial banks' Advisory Committee, a "Brady-type" debt restructuring agreement was signed on February 14, 1994. The agreement, which covered 99 percent of the debt owed to commercial banks, allowed for a reduction of nearly 60 percent in outstanding claims from US$1,251 million to US$520 million (Table 14). The deal was implemented on August 30, 1994 with the purchase by the central bank of 30-year zero-coupon U.S. treasury bonds to serve as collateral for part of the restructured debt.

The agreement provided three options for banks to restructure outstanding principal. Eligible debt, which amounted to US$764 million, could either be

---

Table 14. Summary of the 1994 Restructuring of Commercial Bank Debt
(In millions of U.S. dollars)

	Principal	Interest	Total
Outstanding debt prior to restructuring	776	475	1,251
Debt not included in restructuring	12	5	17
Obligations repurchased	259	96	355
Discount (75 percent of face value)	194	72	266
Cash payment	65	24	89
Principal exchanged for new securities	505	...	505
Discount (35 percent of face value)	177	...	177
New collateralized bonds	329	...	329
Interest restructured	...	374	374
Discount (interest forgiven)	...	141	141
Cash payment (12.5 percent of initial interest)[1]	...	41	41
Past-due interest capitalized	...	191	191
Outstanding debt after restructuring	329	191	520
Total discount	371	213	585
Total cash payments	65	65	130
Plus purchase of collateral[2]	n.a.	n.a.	39
Total cash outlay	**n.a.**	**n.a.**	**169**

Source: BCRD.
[1]Initial interest defined as total past due included in restructuring less interest.
[2]Thirty-year zero-coupon U.S. treasury bonds with face value of US$329 million.

repurchased at a 75 percent discount, exchanged for new collateralized 30-year bonds with an interest rate of LIBOR plus ¹³⁄₁₆ percent offered at a 35 percent discount, or exchanged for new bonds at par with reduced interest rate coupons. The banks' initial choices, however, did not yield a sufficient discount, so they were requested to tender at least 35 percent of outstanding principal for the discounted buyback option.[35] Given the lack of interest in the reduced interest rate bonds, this option was withdrawn in the final settlement.

Nearly all of past-due interest (PDI) at the time of the final settlement was included in the debt restructuring agreement. Of this, US$141 million (30 percent) was forgiven, while US$41 million (12½ percent of the balance) was paid in cash. Similar to the restructuring of principal, one-third of the remaining obligations (US$96 million) were made available for repurchase at a 75 percent discount, with the rest (US$191 million) being capitalized into a new security. The terms of these PDI bonds included a repayment period of 15 years—25 semiannual installments, following a 2½-year grace period, at a yield of LIBOR plus ¹³⁄₁₆ percent. The first seven of these installments were reduced to 1 percent of the original face value, with the remaining 93 percent of the outstanding debt being paid in 18 equal installments, starting in 2001.

The final settlement of the commercial bank debt restructuring involved a total cash outlay of US$169 million by the central bank, which also became the institution liable for servicing the new securities. In addition to the US$41 million of interest paid in cash, US$89 million was used to buy back discounted interest and principal. In addition, a cost of US$39 million was incurred for the purchase of collateral for US$329 million in newly issued discount bonds. Overall, the total discount granted to the Dominican Republic was US$585 million, or 47 percent of the initial obligations to commercial banks. Furthermore, the arrangement made current all obligations to commercial banks, compared with US$1 billion in arrears to commercial banks at the end of 1993.

Evolution of Payments Arrears in 1990–2000

As the economy of the Dominican Republic weakened in 1990, payment arrears nearly doubled from about US$735 million at the end of 1989 to US$1.45 billion at the end of 1990 (Table 12). About half of these new arrears were due to Paris Club members. Following rescheduling and the settlement of non-

rescheduluble arrears to the Paris Club, total arrears fell to about US$779 million at the end of 1991. Debt reduction arrangements with Mexico and Venezuela in 1992 further reduced arrears, but then they jumped to over US$1.25 billion in 1993 in the run-up to the restructuring agreement with the commercial banks.

The 1994 restructuring with commercial banks allowed the Dominican Republic to reduce arrears by over US$1 billion to about US$250 million at the end of 1995, half of which were owed to the CCC and US$100 million to suppliers mainly from Japan, Italy, and Taiwan Province of China. The authorities' efforts to clear these arrears materialized in the 1997 agreements with the CCC and various private suppliers. This reduced the outstanding amount to US$63 million at the end of 1997; by the end of 1998, there were no more arrears.

Past, Present, and Future Debt-Service Payments

The Dominican Republic succeeded in considerably lowering its external debt burden over the 1990s thanks to good macroeconomic policies and strong growth performance. Some disbursements were limited by a lack of counterpart funds. New borrowing was effectively contained by a policy of avoiding reliance on foreign financing and by limited access to international capital markets. Medium- and long-term debt service due has fallen from US$801 million a year at the beginning of the decade to US$405 million in 1999, reflecting a steady decline in principal and interest payments; the debt-service ratio dropped from 12.8 percent in 1990 to 2.3 percent in 1999.

In 1998, after Hurricane Georges hit the Dominican Republic, an informal agreement was reached with the Paris Club, which agreed to tolerate arrears for a rolling six-month period beginning in the last quarter of 1998 and ending in December 1999. By mid-2000 all delayed debt service had been paid, explaining part of the higher debt-service payments in the first half of 2000. Total debt service paid in 2000 is estimated to have risen to US$510 million.

Debt-service payments are expected to increase significantly in 2001 to around US$770 million as a result of (1) the end of the grace period in 2000 of part of the 1991 Paris Club rescheduling, (2) stepped-up payments to commercial banks, which began in 2000, and similar repayments on the restructured arrears with the CCC, (3) debt service on short medium-term bilateral loans at nonconcessional terms contracted in 1999–2000, and (4) the elimination of technical past-due payments that were still within in the grace period at the end of 2000. These obligations are expected to increase debt-service

---

[35]In the final settlement, just under 35 percent of outstanding principal was made available for the discounted buybacks.

payments by about 1 percentage point of GDP to 3.5 percent of GDP in 2001.

External Debt Policy

The approval process for external debt plays an important role in containing its level and composition. The first stage consists of identifying potential projects that can be externally financed. In the second stage, projects are linked to a specific source of external funding, and financial and technical analysis is carried out to determine economic viability. In the third stage, the loan is formalized, documentation is signed, and funds are committed. Finally, the loan must be approved by the central bank and congress (if there is a public guarantee), and promulgated by the executive branch. This last stage, which is generally politicized, has often delayed, or altogether prevented, the finalization of loan documents.

As a result of the extensive use of external debt rescheduling and relief, the Dominican Republic ended the 1990s with one of the lowest external debt burdens in the region and a favorable debt-service profile. Debt to official creditors increased from about 70 percent of total debt at the end of 1993 to 82 percent at the end of 1999, with new loans since 1998 coming mainly from bilateral and multilateral lenders, in particular the IDB and the World Bank. The Dominican Republic used to contract most of its external debt on a medium- and long-term basis. Short-term debt consists mainly of (1) revolving trade lines of credit; and (2) reserve liabilities of the Central Bank and the state-owned commercial bank, *Banco de Reservas.* Nevertheless, as a result of deficiencies in the control and monitoring of public external borrowing, the maturity profile of external debt has lately been deteriorating, with an increasing proportion falling due in the short to medium term at market conditions.

Conclusion

The Dominican Republic availed itself successfully of the benefits of a series of comprehensive debt restructurings and relief in the 1990s. The country managed to grow out of the stifling external debt situation of the 1980s, as a result of high economic growth, which was based on strong export performance and was financed largely from other, nondebt-creating sources. Reliance on external financing was also limited by congressional approval procedures for new loans and by restricted access to international markets resulting from below-investment-grade international credit ratings. Despite progress in reducing the external debt burden to one of the lowest levels in the region, some deficiencies in debt management persisted.

The authorities are working to overhaul public debt management policies and practices, using modern financial techniques to contain the debt-service burden and lower financing costs, in line with the Dominican authorities' aim of smoothing the debt-service profile. This, together with the implementation of sound macroeconomic policies, should help to achieve an upgrade in international credit rankings from the specialized rating agencies.

IV   A Review of Fiscal Policy During the 1990s and Current Policy Considerations

The New Economic Program adopted in late 1990 established fiscal discipline through a comprehensive tax reform and expenditure controls, and paved the way for an extended period of strong economic growth and macroeconomic stability. Moreover, the New Economic Program reduced economic distortions and initiated a shift in the tax base toward more stable, broad-based domestic taxes on income and consumption. Although there were some slippages during the mid-1990s, and a lack of political consensus slowed down the reform process, fiscal discipline was generally maintained over the latter part of the decade. In particular, substantial improvements in administration lifted tax collection to 15 percent of GDP by 1998, the highest level in more than 20 years.

At the end of 2000, facing deteriorating public finances, the authorities accelerated the process of fiscal reforms: administrative discretion was removed from the setting of domestic fuel taxes, external tariffs were reduced, and the tax code was streamlined. Furthermore, in order to enhance transparency in the management of public funds and to tighten fiscal control mechanisms, an integrated financial program was started with the support of the IDB. These steps are intended to enhance public savings, while still allowing increased spending on priority areas, including health, education, and basic infrastructure.

Contribution of Fiscal Policy to Macroeconomic Stability During the 1990s

The monetization of fiscal deficits is a leading cause of high growth in monetary aggregates and of high inflation, which is a serious deterrent to economic growth. During the 1980s, the Dominican Republic fell into this trap. Overall public sector deficits remained high throughout the decade, averaging almost 6 percent of GDP per year, including the quasi-fiscal losses of the central bank.[36] When

external financing of these deficits largely dried up in the early part of the decade, the recourse to domestic financing, primarily from the state-owned commercial bank, *Banco de Reservas,* quickly led to an excessive monetary expansion.[37] In turn, this set off an acceleration in inflation, which contributed to exchange rate pressures, a loss of official international reserves, and an accumulation of external payments arrears. During 1984–90, annual inflation averaged over 35 percent, peaking at 80 percent during 1990, despite at least one short-lived attempt to stabilize the economy in 1985. Institutional and economic rigidities, such as price controls, exacerbated the disruptions to the economy, with annual real GDP growth during this same period averaging less than 2 percent, including a plunge of nearly 6 percent in 1990.

In contrast to the previous decade, the generally disciplined fiscal policy position assumed during the 1990s played a central role in creating a stable macroeconomic environment that was conducive to high economic growth rates. Domestic bank financing of the public sector was reduced, monetary expansion slowed, and annual inflation rates were held to single digits for nearly all of the 1990s (Figure 3). More specifically, the initial stabilization effort embedded in the New Economic Program shifted the overall public sector balance from a deficit of about 7 percent of GDP in 1989 to balance in 1992 (Table 15). This, along with other important structural adjustments included in the program,[38] helped reverse the economic deterioration, with real GDP growing by 1 percent and inflation falling to just under 8 percent during 1991, followed by 8 percent real GDP growth and 5 percent inflation during 1992. Following this strong initial stabilization, aside from some

---

[36]The analysis of fiscal developments in the Dominican Republic is hampered by the poor quality of data. In some years, discrep-ancies between the above-the-line balance and identified financ-ing are very large. Throughout the paper, it is assumed that nega-tive discrepancies identified unrecorded expenditure while posi-tive discrepancies are treated as an accumulation of domestic arrears.

[37]The *Banco de Reservas* maintains roughly a 100 percent re-serve on government deposits in the BCRD. Financing from this bank is equivalent to an expansion of net credit to the nonfinancial public sector by the central bank.

[38]See Chapter I, *Stabilization and Structural Reforms.*

Figure 3. The Overall Public Sector, Net Domestic Bank Credit to Public Sector, and Inflation

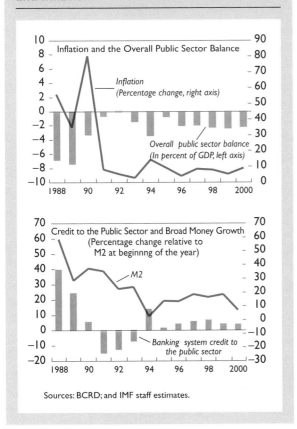

Sources: BCRD; and IMF staff estimates.

slippages associated with the political crisis in 1994,[39] the overall public sector deficit remained under control. During 1993–2000, the deficit generally remained less than 2½ percent of GDP, annual real GDP growth averaged about 6 percent, and inflation (end-period basis) averaged about 7½ percent a year.

The 1990–92 stabilization effort was achieved mainly through tight expenditure controls and strengthened tax revenues. All fiscal operations, including the discretionary spending of the presidency, were placed under a strict cash management system. A swing of 3½ percentage points of GDP (from a deficit of 3½ percent of GDP in 1990 to a balanced budget in 1992) was achieved in the public sector accounts. The latter encompass off-budget revenues,

unidentified discretionary spending, and the overall balance of the nonconsolidated public enterprises. Government tax revenues climbed by nearly 3½ percent of GDP between 1990 and 1992 (Table 16). Most important, increases of 200–300 percent in the state-controlled price of petroleum derivatives during late 1990 resulted in a sharp increase in annual revenues from fuel taxes (the so-called petroleum differential), to about 2 percent of GDP in 1991–92 from virtually zero in 1990.[40] Revenue from customs duties rose by about 1½ percent of GDP in 1992, as imports surged with the improvement in the economy and the liberalization of tariffs. Equally important, however, was the switch to a market-based exchange rate for valuing customs duties, instead of the previously overvalued official rate. The increase in the VAT rate from 6 percent to 8 percent in 1992 also lifted revenue by about ½ percent of GDP.

The large increase in tax revenue and a reduction in net off-budget spending allowed for some increases in budgetary spending without disrupting the stabilization effort. In particular, capital spending increased by about 2 percent of GDP between 1990 and 1993. Reductions relative to GDP in the government wage bill and interest on external debt (mainly due to debt relief received from Venezuela, Mexico, and Paris Club members) ameliorated the impact of the increase in capital expenditure on total spending. In addition, the operational balance of the public enterprises was brought to near zero by 1992, compared with operational losses of about ½ percent of GDP in 1990.

As noted above, there was a temporary deterioration in the fiscal accounts in 1994, as the overall public sector deficit jumped to more than 3 percent of GDP. Election year pressures weakened the cash management system as government spending, particularly capital spending, rose and a net off-budget deficit reemerged for the first time since 1990. Moreover, revenues fell, mainly due to administrative problems in the customs area.

The setback in 1994 was only temporary. Due to a lack of political consensus, however, the overall public sector deficit had initially to be brought under control again through spending restraint and administrative measures. In 1995, the overall public sector deficit was again reduced sharply, to less than 1 percent of GDP, this time through significant cuts in central government capital spending. Tax revenue remained weak, however, falling further to only 13 percent of GDP in 1996, the lowest level since the start of the stabilization program. Customs revenue collection continued to fall and a surge in international

---

[39]The result of the 1994 presidential election was disputed, which contributed to a major capital outflow and loss in official reserves. The main political parties resolved the issue by declaring the sitting President Joaquín Balaguer the winner for a shortened two-year term. The constitution was also amended to bar the re-election of a president for consecutive terms.

[40]These price increases coincided with rising world oil prices during the buildup to the Gulf War. Domestic fuel prices were left unchanged, even when world prices fell in early 1991.

Table 15. Summary of the Consolidated Public Sector
(In percent of GDP)

	1980–89	1990	1991	1992	1993	1994	1995	1996	1997	1998	1999	Prel. 2000
Total revenue	**23.4**	**19.6**	**20.1**	**22.1**	**22.4**	**21.2**	**20.8**	**20.6**	**22.8**	**22.9**	**22.5**	**21.7**
Current revenue[1]	23.0	19.2	19.9	21.8	22.0	21.1	20.0	19.4	21.4	21.6	21.3	21.0
Capital revenue[2]	0.4	0.3	0.2	0.3	0.4	0.1	0.9	1.2	1.4	1.3	1.2	0.7
Total expenditure	**25.6**	**20.4**	**21.0**	**22.2**	**24.1**	**24.4**	**20.9**	**22.2**	**24.1**	**23.9**	**23.7**	**23.5**
Current expenditure	19.3	13.4	12.8	13.6	14.1	14.6	12.8	13.9	17.1	17.2	18.0	19.0
Capital expenditure	6.3	7.1	8.2	8.7	10.0	9.8	8.1	8.3	7.0	6.7	5.7	4.6
Current account balance	3.8	5.9	7.0	8.3	7.8	6.6	7.2	5.4	4.3	4.4	3.3	2.0
General government	4.8	6.5	7.2	8.3	7.7	7.1	7.4	6.3	5.9	5.3	4.4	3.3
Public enterprises	−1.0	−0.6	−0.2	0.0	0.2	−0.5	−0.3	−0.9	−1.6	−0.9	−1.1	−1.2
Central bank losses	**−1.1**	**0.0**	**0.0**	**0.0**	**0.0**	**−0.5**	**−0.4**	**−0.6**	**−0.7**	**−0.5**	**−0.4**	**−0.4**
Unidentified expenditure[2]	**−3.2**	**−2.5**	...	...	...	...	**−0.5**	...	**−0.2**	**−0.9**	**−1.1**	**−0.2**
Overall balance before grants	**−6.5**	**−3.4**	**−0.9**	**−0.1**	**−1.8**	**−3.6**	**−1.0**	**−2.2**	**−2.2**	**−2.4**	**−2.7**	**−2.5**
Grants	**0.8**	**0.1**	**0.2**	**0.2**	**0.3**	**0.2**	**0.3**	**0.2**	**0.2**	**0.3**	**0.3**	**0.2**
Overall balance after grants	**−5.8**	**−3.3**	**−0.7**	**0.1**	**−1.4**	**−3.4**	**−0.7**	**−2.1**	**−2.0**	**−2.1**	**−2.5**	**−2.2**
Financing	**5.8**	**3.3**	**0.7**	**−0.1**	**1.4**	**3.4**	**0.7**	**2.1**	**2.0**	**2.1**	**2.5**	**2.2**
Foreign	2.3	2.5	1.5	0.7	0.1	−0.9	−0.1	−0.2	−0.4	0.0	0.8	0.4
Domestic	3.4	0.8	−0.8	−0.8	1.3	4.3	0.8	2.3	2.3	2.1	1.7	1.9
Of which												
Bank financing[3]	3.4	0.8	−2.0	−2.0	−1.3	2.9	0.3	0.9	1.2	1.6	1.0	1.1
Memorandum items:												
Primary balance	−4.0	−0.8	1.6	1.9	0.6	−2.1	0.6	−0.9	−1.0	−1.2	−1.6	−1.3

Sources: National Budget Office (ONAPRE); BCRD; and IMF staff estimates.
[1]Net of intrapublic sector transector transfers.
[2]Equal to the difference between the above-the-line balance and the identified financing. Positive values are treated as an accumulation of domestic arrears and added to the domestic financing.
[3]Includes the financing of the central bank's quasi-fiscal losses.

Table 16. Summary Operations of the Central Government
(In percent of GDP)

	1980–89	1990	1991	1992	1993	1994	1995	1996	1997	1998	1999	Prel. 2000
Total revenue	13.1	12.4	13.5	15.2	15.7	14.7	14.9	14.1	16.2	15.9	15.9	15.9
Current revenue	13.0	12.1	13.3	15.0	15.5	14.6	14.8	13.9	15.9	15.9	15.6	15.8
Tax revenue²	11.4	10.3	11.7	13.7	14.6	13.6	13.4	12.9	14.7	15.0	14.7	14.7
Taxes on income and profits	2.4	2.6	2.4	2.4	2.5	2.3	2.5	2.5	3.0	3.2	3.4	3.4
Taxes on property	0.1	0.1	0.1	0.1	0.1	0.1	0.1	0.1	0.2	0.2	0.3	0.3
Taxes on goods and services	3.9	3.4	5.1	5.4	6.4	6.7	6.6	6.4	7.0	7.2	6.1	5.5
Of which												
Oil price differential	1.2	0.2	2.3	1.9	2.3	2.5	2.1	1.8	2.4	2.6	1.5	1.0
Value-added tax (ITBIS)	0.7	1.6	1.5	2.1	2.6	2.6	2.5	2.5	2.9	3.0	3.1	3.1
Taxes on international trade	4.8	4.1	4.0	5.7	5.5	4.4	4.0	3.8	4.2	4.3	4.8	5.3
Of which												
Foreign exch. commission	...	...	...	...	...	...	...	...	...	...	0.3	1.0
Other taxes	0.2	0.1	0.1	0.1	0.1	0.1	0.1	0.1	0.2	0.1	0.2	0.2
Non-tax revenue	1.6	1.8	1.6	1.3	0.9	1.0	1.4	1.1	1.2	0.9	0.9	1.1
Capital revenue	0.1	0.3	0.2	0.2	0.2	0.1	0.1	0.2	0.3	0.1	0.3	0.0
Grants	0.8	0.1	0.2	0.2	0.3	0.2	0.1	0.1	0.1	0.2	0.1	0.1
Total expenditure	14.8	13.6	14.0	15.7	18.5	18.4	15.4	16.1	17.4	17.0	18.2	17.5
Current expenditure	9.7	7.5	7.4	7.8	9.1	8.4	8.1	8.8	11.7	12.0	12.9	13.2
Wages and salaries	4.2	2.7	2.3	2.5	2.9	3.1	3.5	3.6	4.6	5.3	5.1	5.6
Goods and services	1.6	1.0	0.9	1.4	1.8	2.1	1.4	1.6	0.6	1.8	1.7	1.6
Interest	1.0	1.6	1.6	1.2	1.6	1.0	1.1	0.9	0.7	0.7	0.7	0.8
Current transfers¹	3.0	1.9	1.6	1.6	2.2	1.7	2.1	2.7	3.7	3.6	3.7	3.4
Other²	0.0	0.2	1.0	1.0	0.6	0.5	0.1	0.1	2.0	0.6	1.7	1.8
Capital expenditure	5.1	6.1	6.6	7.9	9.4	10.0	7.3	7.3	5.7	5.0	5.3	4.2
Fixed investment²	2.4	3.4	2.4	3.5	5.4	6.0	5.0	5.4	3.8	2.9	3.0	2.9
Capital transfers³	2.3	2.4	3.2	3.4	3.4	3.5	2.2	1.9	1.6	1.8	2.0	1.1
Other	0.4	0.2	1.0	1.0	0.6	0.5	0.1	0.1	0.3	0.2	0.3	0.2
Current account balance⁴	3.3	4.6	5.9	7.2	6.4	6.2	6.7	5.1	4.2	3.8	2.7	2.6
Unrecorded expenditure⁵	-1.8	-0.2	0.0	0.0	0.0	0.0	0.0	0.0	-0.1	-0.2	0.0	-0.6
Overall balance	-2.6	-1.3	-0.3	-0.2	-2.4	-3.5	-0.4	-2.0	-1.2	-1.1	-2.2	-2.1
Financing	2.6	1.3	0.3	0.2	2.4	3.5	0.4	2.0	1.2	1.1	2.2	2.1
Foreign	1.4	1.6	1.1	0.5	0.4	-0.4	0.2	0.1	-0.4	0.1	0.9	0.5
Domestic	1.2	-0.2	-0.8	-0.3	2.0	3.9	0.1	1.9	1.6	1.0	1.3	1.6
Banking system	1.1	-0.2	-1.7	-1.7	-0.7	1.6	-0.9	0.5	0.5	0.5	0.6	0.8
Domestic arrears (net change)	0.1	0.0	1.0	1.4	2.6	2.3	0.9	1.5	0.5	0.4	0.5	-0.6
Private sector⁶	0.0	0.0	0.0	0.0	0.0	0.0	0.2	0.0	0.6	0.1	0.2	1.4

Sources: ONAPRE; the BCRD; and IMF staff estimates.

[1] Includes notional transfers to public enterprises to service interest payments on their external debt.

[2] Includes extrabudgetary expenditures not reported by ONAPRE.

[3] Includes notional transfers to public enterprises to service amortization payments on their external debt.

[4] Excluding grants.

[5] Equal to the difference between the above-the-line balance and the identified financing. Positive values are treated as an accumulation of domestic arrears and added to the domestic financing.

[6] Reflect net payments deferred to the following year.

oil prices cut deeply into revenue from the petroleum differential. At the end of 1996, the authorities had also raised domestic fuel prices to strengthen revenues from the petroleum differential. During 1997–98, a concerted effort to improve tax administration through automation of customs, creation of large taxpayer units, tough penalties for late payment (following a brief amnesty period), and cross-checking devices enabled tax collection to climb to a new high of 15 percent of GDP by 1998, with no major changes to the tax law.

Since the spending cuts in 1995, central government current expenditures have climbed sharply relative to GDP, rising to 12 percent of GDP in 1998 from nearly 9 percent of GDP in 1996. An increase of roughly 50 percent in public sector wages from March 1, 1997, and a steady increase in current transfers, mostly to the public sector,[41] were largely responsible for the rise in current spending. In 1998, some curbs on this spending growth were implemented, such as a freeze on public sector wages, but hurricane-related spending during the fourth quarter negated earlier efforts to reduce current spending during the year.

Growth in total government spending was moderated, however, by cutbacks in capital spending. Between 1996 and 1998, capital spending fell by about 2½ percent of GDP from earlier, excessive levels, when the outgoing government hurried to complete some major construction projects before leaving office in 1996.

In mid-1999, the fiscal situation started deteriorating. Election-related expenditure overruns were compounded by delays in adjusting domestic fuel prices in line with increasing international oil prices, resulting in dramatically reduced government proceeds from the oil differential. In October 1999, growing difficulties in servicing the external debt induced the Monetary Board to raise the foreign exchange commission from 1.75 percent to 5 percent,[42] and the government raised domestic fuel prices by about 20 percent on average.[43] Despite this measure, the central government deficit widened by one percentage point of GDP to more than 2 percent of GDP. The overall consolidated public sector deficit widened marginally to 2½ percent of GDP, but fell short of the authorities' original target of near balance. The fiscal slippages contributed to put upward pressure on domestic demand and prices, and in turn on the external current account.

Reflecting a rapid pace of government expenditure, the central government deficit continued to widen in the first half of 2000, reaching almost 4 percent of GDP. The new administration, sworn in on August 16, reacted to worsening fiscal conditions by implementing severe expenditure controls, increasing domestic fuel prices,[44] and eventually introducing a new hydrocarbon law that removed administrative discretion in the setting of domestic fuel prices. As a result, by the end of 2000, the central government had narrowed its deficit to some 2 percent of GDP.

Another development in recent years, since the relaxation of the cash management system, has been the accumulation of domestic arrears, mainly to contractors and suppliers. The lack of transparency in the budget process, together with limited coordination between revenue and spending agencies allowed domestic arrears to accumulate. In the second half of 1999, congress approved a law that allowed the conversion into marketable government securities of arrears accumulated before August 1995. A commission was set up to assess claimants' rights.[45] However, domestic arrears continued to accumulate. Information is still incomplete, although it is roughly estimated that at mid-2000, domestic arrears may have totaled some 3½ percent of GDP.[46]

Tax Reform and Administration

The tax system in the Dominican Republic went through two major reforms: the first one at the beginning of the 1990s and the second at the end of 2000. The tax reform of 1990–92 had to be comprehensive in order to correct a tax system of immense complexity that had lost much of its revenue-generating capacity due to high inflation in the late 1980s and 1990. The reform encompassed taxes on international trade, personal and corporate income taxes, VAT, and excise taxes. The tax reform was successful in gradually shifting the tax burden to the broad-based income tax and VAT, and thus securing a more stable revenue base with growth potential. Toward the end of 2000, in order to address the deterioration in public finances and to compensate for foreseen revenue losses associated with a planned reduction in external tariffs, the VAT and some excise taxes were

---

[41]In addition to the transfers to public enterprises, current government transfers largely reflect wage payments in the decentralized agencies of the general government.

[42]The first 1.75 percentage points continued to be retained by the central bank while the remainder was transferred to the central government and mainly earmarked to cover external debt service.

[43]Domestic fuel prices had remained unchanged since March 1998. Subsidies for the domestic use of propane gas were preserved.

---

[44]In August, domestic fuel prices were raised by about 30 percent on average.

[45]The approved law allowed the government to issue bonds for RD$5 billion (about 2 percent of 1999 GDP) with a six-year maturity and a 7 percent interest rate.

[46]In this regard, the government established a domestic debt commission in December 2000 to help evaluate this issue.

raised, a minimum tax on gross sales was introduced, and the domestic fuel tax system was reformed.

The tariff reform initiated in September 1990 addressed numerous problems in the existing system.[47] As noted in Chapter II, *Trade Reform Continues,* the tariff reform simplified customs duties by reducing the number of tariff rates from well over 100 to 8, ranging from 5 percent to 35 percent,[48] and eliminating an array of specific import taxes. While this represented a sharp reduction in the maximum tariff rate (from over 100 percent), average tariffs were still high by regional standards and the tariff structure allowed for a continuation of high rates of effective protection for domestic industries. Also, concomitant with the tariff reform, the authorities imposed new selective consumption taxes on various import items with rates of 5–80 percent. As a result, despite having taken a major step forward, the Dominican Republic still retained a relatively restrictive trade regime. The reform did, however, eliminate export taxes.

The new tax code issued in May 1992 (Law 11–92) modified domestic taxes in a profound way. For the personal income tax, it reduced marginal income tax rates substantially, with the maximum rate falling initially from 70 percent to 30 percent and then to 25 percent by 1995. The number of tax brackets was reduced to 3 from 16 with tax rates of 15 percent and 20 percent applied to the lower brackets. The level of minimum taxable income was raised (to about three to four times the minimum wage), effectively exempting 90 percent of wage earners from the income tax, thus greatly enhancing tax progressivity and simplifying administration. Tax brackets were also adjusted annually for inflation during the previous year and most tax deductions were eliminated.

The corporate income tax underwent similar reforms. The tax rate was lowered from 46 percent to 30 percent in 1992 and then to 25 percent by 1995, which not only reduced the disincentives to formalizing operations, but also harmonized the corporate income tax with the personal income tax.[49] The reform also introduced mechanisms to adjust the tax base for inflation, eliminated the double taxation of dividend income, and expanded tax coverage.

The new tax code also raised consumption taxes. In particular, the VAT rate was raised from 6 percent to 8 percent and various excise taxes were converted from specific to ad valorem taxes, after having lost much of their effectiveness due to the previously high rates of inflation.

The tax reform has been successful, albeit gradually, in shifting the tax burden to the more stable, broad-based domestic taxes with improved revenue growth potential. That is, the share of total tax revenue generated by the income tax and VAT grew from about 33 percent in 1992 to 44 percent in 2000 (Table 17). As a share of total tax revenue, revenue from import duties fell sharply between 1992 and 1995, before leveling off at 29 percent.[50] Revenue from the petroleum differential, in contrast, has averaged about 15 percent of total tax revenue, but its variation has been substantial, ranging from 14 percent to 19 percent of total tax revenue during 1991–98.

The structure of petroleum taxation in force until end-2000 made it susceptible to large swings in revenue-generating capacity. The tax was determined as the difference between the pump price of various fuels (gasoline, diesel, kerosene, aviation fuel, fuel oil, and propane gas),[51] which were controlled by the state, less their ex-refinery price and a distributor's margin. The ex-refinery price varied directly with international oil prices and changed in the official exchange rate.[52] The pump prices, however, were seldom adjusted, so that a fall in world prices provided a boost to revenues, while an exchange rate depreciation or an increase in world prices reduced revenues. For example, fuel prices were left essentially unchanged between late 1990 and late 1996, at which time higher international oil prices and a devaluation of the peso cut deeply into revenues. Although a price adjustment mechanism was then incorporated into the differential's regulations, it was used infrequently, and mostly for price decreases.

Following the 1994 presidential election and strong gains by the opposition in the legislature in the 1996 election, the tax reform process slowed as the political climate became more difficult. Thus, prior to the administration of President Mejía, the tax code had been left essentially unchanged since the mid-1990s.[53]

After the 2000 presidential election, the new government, facing a deteriorating fiscal situation, put forward a package of fiscal reforms, including a new hydrocarbons tax law and several changes to the tax code that were approved by congress toward

---

[47]The tariff reform was initially announced by decree in 1990 (Law 339–90) and finally set into law in September 1993. An exchange surcharge of 15 percent that was applied to about 40 percent of imports was gradually eliminated by June 1995.

[48]Since then, two additional tariff rates of 0 and 3 percent have been introduced.

[49]The ten tax brackets that existed previously were also unified.

[50]Revenues from taxes on international trade climbed to over 32 percent of total tax revenue in 1999–2000, reflecting the increase in the foreign exchange commission.

[51]The differential for propane is actually a subsidy (that is, it is negative).

[52]The public/private joint venture national refinery (Refidomsa) essentially has monopoly rights to import petroleum products. It obtains its foreign exchange for these imports at the official exchange rate.

[53]In 1998, taxes on business licenses and assets of financial institutions (*patentes*) were eliminated and taxes on international telephone calls were reduced.

Table 17. Tax Revenue by Source
(In percent of total tax revenue)

	1990	1991	1992	1993	1994	1995	1996	1997	1998	1999	Prel. 2000
Total tax revenue	**100.0**	**100.0**	**100.0**	**100.0**	**100.0**	**100.0**	**100.0**	**100.0**	**100.0**	**100.0**	**100.0**
Taxes on income and profits	25.6	20.9	17.8	17.4	17.1	19.0	19.5	20.8	21.3	23.3	23.4
Taxes on property	1.0	0.7	0.7	0.7	0.8	0.8	0.9	1.5	1.6	1.9	1.9
Taxes on goods and services	33.3	43.5	39.7	43.6	49.2	49.7	49.8	47.6	48.0	41.2	37.0
Of which											
Oil price differential	1.5	19.9	14.2	15.6	18.3	15.7	14.3	16.6	17.3	10.2	6.6
VAT	15.6	13.0	15.6	18.0	18.8	18.9	19.6	19.8	19.8	20.9	20.8
Taxes on international trade[1]	39.4	34.4	41.4	37.7	32.4	30.0	29.4	28.6	28.6	32.5	36.2
Other taxes	0.7	0.5	0.4	0.6	0.5	0.5	0.5	1.6	0.4	1.1	1.5
Memorandum item:											
Broad-based domestic taxes[2]	41.2	33.9	33.4	35.4	36.0	37.9	39.1	40.6	41.1	44.2	44.2

Sources: ONAPRE; and the BCRD.
[1] Starting 1999, it includes proceeds from the increase in the foreign exchange commission.
[2] Consists of income taxes and VAT.

the end of 2000, together with a reduction in external tariffs.[54]

The new hydrocarbons law converted the previous system of fuel price differentials into an array of specific excise taxes (indexed to the CPI). Administrative discretion was thus removed and retail prices started being revised weekly in line with wholesale prices. This reform will help to reduce the volatility of government revenues.

A number of changes to the tax code were also made. In particular, the VAT rate was raised to 12 percent—closer to the average in Latin America—and its base was enlarged to include a number of services previously subjected to specific taxes. About half of the economy's value added continues, however, to be exempt, thus limiting revenues and complicating administration. Excise taxes on alcoholic beverages and cigarettes were also increased by 5–30 percentage points and a minimum tax of 1.5 percent on gross sales was introduced, with an exception for companies with gross sales of less than RD$2 million a year (about US$120,000).[55]

Considerable advances have been achieved in the area of tax administration in recent years. In 1997, an automated system for customs administration was implemented at the major air and seaports. This system greatly reduced the discretion of customs officers in administering import duties, which was a major source of revenue losses and potential corruption. Since 1996, customs revenues have increased by ½ percent of GDP. With regard to imports of large items, such as vehicles, machinery and equipment, and large consumer durables, the customs administration has been building the capacity to cross-check information with income tax and VAT to ensure consistency in taxpayers' declarations of these taxes.

To facilitate the coordination of domestic taxes, the administrative agency for income taxes was combined with the agency responsible for VAT and other domestic taxes to form the *Dirección General de Impuestos Internos* (DGII) in 1996. The first priority of the DGII was to establish a large taxpayer unit for the capital district, which was accomplished in late 1997, with about 450 registered taxpayers. These taxpayers would be subject to a full tax audit at least once every three years. The authorities have also made a strong effort to register all taxpayers, big and small, with a unique identity code. As a result of these efforts, and the development of the cross-checking system, tax collection (particularly from VAT) from small and medium-sized firms has also been growing rapidly. To encourage voluntary compliance with the tax code

and taxpayer registration, the government offered a temporary tax amnesty in 1997, which was followed by the enforcement of stiff penalties, such as a penalty interest rate of 25 percent a month for late payment. Tax administration is still hampered, however, by the existence of numerous small taxes and fees, which generate little or no revenue.[56]

Reforming the Budget Process and Redirecting Public Expenditure

Recently, the authorities have begun to reform the budget process, which currently lacks transparency and accountability. The Office of the Presidency maintains discretionary spending accounts that are generally free from congressional oversight. Although the last administration reduced the use of these accounts, discretional spending still accounts for about 20 percent of total government spending (down from about 50 percent under previous administrations).

Revenue is directed to these discretionary accounts through two main sources. First, as part of the budget process, a revenue target for the upcoming year is determined. Any revenue collected during the course of the year in excess of this amount becomes available to the Office of the Presidency (through account 1401). Second, the budget approved by congress sets maximum spending limits on each item. If spending is held below these limits, the unspent resources are also redirected to discretionary accounts. If congress fails to approve the administration's budget proposal, the revenue estimates and spending limits of the previous budget remain in effect, unadjusted for growth or inflation. These rules create extraordinary leverage for the administration in the approval of the budget, weakening the role of congressional oversight. If congress rejects the administration's proposal, it increases the discretionary funds available to the presidency as tax revenues grow.

Under the present institutional procedures for execution of the budget, slippages in the coordination and control of expenditures may occur,[57] giving rise to domestic arrears. This can happen because the main revenue collection agencies (customs and the DGII) report to the secretary of finance,[58] while the budget office (ONAPRE) reports to the technical secretary of the presidency. The controller's office,

---

[54]The tariff reform narrowed the tariff structure from nine to five non-zero rates and reduced the maximum tariff rate to 20 percent from 35 percent, almost halving the simple average tariff rate to 11 percent.

[55]The fiscal measures were complemented by a temporary tax amnesty on 1999 tax declarations and on pending tax disputes.

[56]A draft law eliminating 11 taxes with marginal proceeds was presented by the new administration, but the approval by the congress is still pending.

[57]During the stabilization effort of the early 1990s, the president himself coordinated revenue and spending operations.

[58]A substantial share of collected revenue, including the petroleum differential and nontax revenues associated with the granting of mining rights, is delivered directly to the national treasury or the office of the presidency.

which is a separate branch of the administration, serves as an intermediary between the two. Thus, over the course of the year, ONAPRE notifies the spending agencies of their spending limits. The agencies then proceed with their spending programs. However, there is no firm commitment by the government to cover these expenses until they are approved by the controller's office. Once a commitment has been approved, however, the national treasury makes payments only if the resources are available. As a result, domestic arrears have accumulated when the coordination between the budget execution agencies has been relaxed. As these arrears have become a regular feature of government operations, procurement costs have risen and the government's creditworthiness has been damaged. The authorities are considering a comprehensive proposal for the modernization of the state, which, in addition to streamlining the public sector and enhancing the efficiency of government operations, would also address the problems in the budget process.

At the end of 2000, congress approved a technical cooperation loan from the IDB to fund an integrated financial management program (IFMP), aimed particularly at making fiscal policy more consistent with national development objectives; strengthening the institutional setting; and increasing transparency in the management of public funds and the effectiveness of internal controls. In order to strengthen policy formulation and improve budget monitoring, policy decisions will be centralized, but the operational execution will be decentralized in the relevant public agencies. The program also aims at (1) enhancing coordination among institutions (Secretariat of Finances, the central bank, and the Technical Secretariat); (2) improving the accounting practices and the information processing system with the goal of producing comprehensive, timely, and reliable information; and (3) strengthening the role of the Office of the Comptroller General through the development of a modern internal control system to analyze budget management from the economic, financial, and legal point of view. The program should improve substantially the financial management capacity of public sector institutions as well as enhancing governance by making management of public funds more transparent and accountable.

The authorities have acknowledged that while the primary approach toward improving social conditions and poverty alleviation is to sustain high real GDP growth rates for the economy, more government resources also need to be directed toward social services, including health and education, and basic infrastructure. During 1998–99, spending on health and education rose to about 4 percent of GDP, compared with just over 3 percent of GDP in 1995. But these spending levels are still low by international standards. It is anticipated that over the medium term spending in these priority areas, as well as on basic infrastructure, could grow by 2–3 percentage points of GDP. The additional spending would come from savings obtained from the reduction in transfers to public enterprises, largely achieved through the ongoing privatization process,[59] and a rationalization of the civil service.

Conclusion

A remarkable fiscal adjustment and comprehensive tax reform during the early 1990s were instrumental in achieving high real GDP growth rates and moderate inflation for the remainder of the decade. Largely due to the difficult political climate that prevailed during the mid-1990s, however, the pace of fiscal reform slowed. Momentum picked up again toward the end of 2000, when a new hydrocarbons tax law and a number of changes to the tax code were approved, and an integrated financial management program was initiated to enhance transparency and accountability in the management of public funds. The IFMP should also foster a rationalization of public expenditure, providing room for augmenting government spending in priority areas, such as health, education, and basic infrastructure, without undermining fiscal discipline.

References

Dauharje, Andrés, hijo, Jaime Aristy Escuder, and others, 1996, *El Programa: Programa Macroeconómico de Mediano Plazo para la República Dominicana: 1996–2000* (Santo Domingo).

Dirección General de Impuestos Internos, 1999, *Proyecto de Simplificación del Sistema Tributario,* (preliminary) (Santo Domingo).

Foreign Tax Law Publishers, 1993, *Tax Laws of the World —Dominican Republic,* (Ormond Beach, Florida).

Lizardo, Magdalena, and Rolando Guzmán, 1999, *La Reforma Arancelaria: Elementos Para su Racionalización,* Oficina Nacional de Planificación, Working Paper.

Oficina Nacional de Planificación, 1998, *La Economía Dominicana: Comportamiento Reciente y Perspectivas de Mediano Plazo* (unpublished) (Santo Domingo).

Oficina Nacional de Presupuesto, 1998, *Informe de Ejecución Presupuestaria 1997* (Santo Domingo).

Pellerano, Fernando, 1999, *Una Evaluación de la Situación Fiscal Dominicana,* Secretaría de Finanzas, Working Paper (Santo Domingo).

World Bank, 1999, *Country Assistance Strategy Paper* of the World Bank Group for the Dominican Republic (Washington: World Bank).

---

[59]See Chapter I for a more thorough discussion of this reform.

V Capital Accumulation, Total Factor Productivity, and Growth

Since the restoration of macroeconomic stability in 1991, the Dominican Republic has entered a period of remarkable economic growth. During the period 1991–98 annual average GDP growth was more than 6 percent (Table 18), with even higher growth rates in recent years. This positive performance came after more than a decade of low and volatile growth dating back to the late 1970s. The resumption of strong economic growth has already had a beneficial impact on poverty and recent analysis by the BCRD indicates that between 1992 and 1998, the incidence[60] of poverty declined from 31.7 percent to 25.8 percent.

With more than 2 million Dominicans still living in poverty, the sustainability of growth is a key issue. There is a dual nature to the production structure that raises questions about the sustainability of current growth rates. On the one hand, there are areas such as tourism, telecommunications, and the industrial FTZs, which operate in a highly competitive environment, are closely linked to the world economy, and

are often shielded from state intervention through special administrative arrangements. On the other hand, there are the more traditional sectors of the economy, such as agriculture and some subsectors of industry (outside the FTZs), which continue to operate amidst strong state intervention, including excessive protectionism, red tape, and insecure property rights. Without continued progress in implementing structural reforms (particularly in the more traditional sectors), sustained growth could be jeopardized.

Sources of Growth in the Dominican Republic

Studying the determinants of growth has been at the core of economic research for half a century. The pioneering study of Solow (1956) on the mechanics of factor accumulation and GDP growth led to a host of applied papers designed to test the applicability of the exogenous growth model, the role of total factor productivity, and the validity of the standard neoclassical production function (for a survey see Maddison,

---

[60]Percentage of population living in conditions of poverty.

Table 18. Economic Structure and Growth, 1991–98

	1991 (In percent of GDP)	1998 (In percent of GDP)	1991–98 Average Annual Growth (In percent)	1991–98 Contribution to Growth (In percent)
Construction	7.5	12.1	13.8	20.7
Commerce	12.4	12.9	6.8	12.5
Hotels, bars, and restaurants	4.2	7.0	14.0	14.3
Industry	14.9	13.1	4.3	7.5
Telecommunications	2.4	4.7	16.5	9.0
Agriculture	13.9	11.7	3.5	6.8
FTZ[1]	3.3	3.4	7.2	5.3
Total economy	100.0	100.0	6.1	100.0

Source: BCRD.
[1]The national accounts methodology does not fully capture the contribution to growth of the FTZs, since it is based only on the wage bill and not on value added.

1987). Most of these studies were based on the notion that economic growth was the outcome of capital and labor accumulation and technological improvements leading to factor productivity growth. Accordingly, it was assumed that value added in each sector could be expressed as:[61]

$$\mathrm{Log}_{Yt} = \gamma + \alpha_1 \mathrm{Log}_{Kt} + \alpha_2 \mathrm{Log}_{Lt} + \mu_t \qquad (1)$$

Because the variables in equation (1) are nonstationary (see unit root tests in Appendix V) parameter estimates using standard techniques (for example, ordinary least squares methods) do not have standard asymptotically normal distributions and are prone to spurious correlations (Granger and Newbold, 1974). This model is therefore best estimated by using cointegration techniques. In addition, since a lack of proper accounting of short-term fluctuations can potentially bias the estimation (Hargreaves, 1994), this basic specification was extended to capture the short-run dynamics of growth arising from the presence of transitory shocks by estimating:

$$\Delta\mathrm{Log}_{Yt} = \alpha_0 \Delta\mathrm{Log}_{Kt} + (1 - \alpha_0)\Delta\mathrm{Log}_{Lt} + \qquad (2)$$
$$\beta[\mathrm{Log}_{Yt-1} - \gamma - \alpha_1\mathrm{Log}_{Kt-1} - (1 - \alpha_1)\mathrm{Log}_{Lt-1}] + \varepsilon_t$$

In this specification, Δ is the first difference of the variables, and the expression in brackets corresponds to the last period's deviation of output from its long-term determinants. For example, from a condition of excess capacity the self-correcting mechanism immediately calls for a future expansion in growth. The speed of the adjustment is determined by β; the smaller the value of β, the slower is the adjustment process. The parameter α_0 captures the short-run effect of capital and labor on the growth rate, while parameter α_1 captures the long-run effect of capital and labor on output. The latter are then used to estimate the contribution of each factor of production to growth with the residual accounting for technology or productivity change.

The model from equation (2) was estimated for the 1970–98 period using annual data, with separate estimates being carried out for the FTZs to capture some of the dual nature of the Dominican economy.[62] The estimates presented in Table 19 indicate that the share of capital in the economy's production function (excluding the FTZs)—at about 63 percent—is similar to factor compensation shares in the

country's national accounts of roughly 65 percent during 1992–97.[63] Surprisingly, the estimated equation for the FTZs does not reflect the conventional thought that the FTZs are more labor intensive than the rest of the economy. Finally, the parameter for the speed of adjustment in each sector, β, suggests that FTZs adjust to shocks about twice as quickly as the rest of the economy (1.5 years versus 3 years).

Sources of Growth Excluding the FTZs

The estimates of sources of growth based on the production function estimates of Table 19 indicate that for the last 25 years, the most important source of growth by far has been capital accumulation. At the same time, there has been a remarkably low contribution of total factor productivity growth to overall economic growth. This result is even stronger when considering that the estimate of labor growth does not take into account improvements in educational attainment that have undoubtedly taken place in the last three decades.[64] Consequently, it could be expected that the unmeasured improvements in human capital are being captured in the form of total factor productivity increases, which nevertheless average only 0.4 percent per year.

Such low overall improvements in productivity should obviously be a source of concern, since they raise doubts about the sustainability of strong growth. However, separating the analysis into different periods (Table 20) provides a somewhat different picture. The strong growth *since 1992* has relied both on capital accumulation and on important growth in total factor productivity. The increase in capital accumulation is attributable to a rebound in savings that has taken place since 1992. The ratio of investment to GDP, which had declined from about 23 percent in the 1970s to 20 percent during the 1982–91 period, has been consistently increasing since 1992, averaging more than 24 percent for the 1992–98 period. By the same token, total factor productivity growth since 1992 has averaged a historically high 2.3 percent per year.

Assessing the determinants of this increase in capital accumulation and total factor productivity growth is beyond the scope of this chapter. However, some important stylized facts are worth mentioning. First, there is a strong correlation between the suc-

---

[61]Equation (1) is derived under the assumption that the production function is Cobb-Douglas. Under constant returns to scale, the estimated parameters of inputs equation (1) are equal to the factor shares in production, while the estimated constant is a proxy (up to a scale) of the average productivity growth. Tests indicated that the null hypothesis of constant returns to scale in both the FTZs and the rest of the economy could not be rejected and the estimation of (1) was carried out under the restriction that $\alpha_1 + \alpha_2 = 1$.

[62]All results must be interpreted with caution, given that GDP data use a base year of 1970. The stock of capital was estimated using the perpetual inventory method (see Appendix V). Reason-

able changes in depreciation rates (from 4 percent to 6 percent) or in the capital-to-GDP ratio (from 2½ to 3) do not affect the results qualitatively, although quantitatively, the coefficient estimates will vary slightly.

[63]These shares are similar to those found by Senhadji (1999) (ranging from 0.52 to 0.72 for Latin American countries).

[64]There are insufficient data on educational attainment to control for this variable.

cessful macroeconomic stabilization of 1991 and the initiation of structural reforms in the early 1990s with the rebound in capital accumulation and total factor productivity growth. Second, the instability associated with the debt crisis of the 1980s not only affected capital accumulation, but also productivity growth. While some of the high productivity growth in the early 1990s may have been attributable to a rebound effect, toward the end of the 1990s this was to

be less of a factor. Nonetheless, the analysis would seem to indicate that sustained strong productivity growth will not be possible without continued implementation of structural reforms. Third, the experience of other developing countries shows that sustaining productivity growth rates of the kind that have been experienced recently by the Dominican Republic is difficult (Table 21). Some of the fastest-growing economies in the world, such as Chile, Ire-

Table 19. Production Function Estimates, 1970–98

Sectors	α_0	α_1	β	γ	R^2 Cointegration*	R^2 Error Correction	DW
Free-trade zones	0.301 (0.212)	0.714 (0.042)	0.907 (0.183)	−4.09 (0.184)	0.980	0.817	2.07
Rest of the economy	0.824 (0.161)	0.632 (0.168)	0.337 (0.122)	−0.355 (0.276)	0.972	0.570	1.99

Note: (*) Corresponds to the sample fit of the cointegrating vector. Standard deviations are in parentheses.

Table 20. Sources of Growth Estimates
(In percent)

Period	GDP Growth (A year)	Capital			Labor			Total Factor Productivity Growth	
		Growth (A year)	Contribution to GDP Growth	Share in GDP Growth	Growth (A year)	Contribution to GDP Growth	Share in GDP Growth	Contribution to GDP Growth	Share in GDP Growth
1973–98	4.6	4.5	2.8	62.3	3.6	1.3	29.2	0.4	8.5
1973–82	5.6	5.3	3.4	59.6	4.1	1.5	26.7	0.8	13.7
1983–91	2.2	3.6	2.3	106.1	3.9	1.4	65.8	−1.6	−71.9
1992–98	6.1	4.4	2.8	45.8	2.6	1.0	15.8	2.3	38.3

Table 21. Total Factor Productivity Growth of Other Developing Countries
(In percent)

	Korea	Taiwan Province of China	Singapore	Chile	Ireland	Morocco	Jordan
1960–70	0.60	1.40	0.10	1.40	2.50	4.60	−1.10
1970–80	0.80	1.10	0.40	0.00	1.70	−0.20	3.00
1980–86	2.50	1.80	−0.80	−1.90	1.20	−0.30	−2.60
1986–92	1.90	2.50	4.00	3.80	3.40	−1.20	−4.30

Source: Bosworth, Collins and Chen, 1995.

land, Korea, and Taiwan Province of China, have not been able to sustain average annual productivity growth rates in excess of 2 percent for more than five or six years.

Sources of Growth for the FTZs

The traditional methodology for estimating sources of growth assumes that the long-run structure of the economy is unaffected by the accumulation of capital and labor and, therefore, the underlying production function remains constant over time. In the presence of important structural reforms and a rapidly expanding sector such as the FTZs, where learning and adaptation is an important process, this may not be a reasonable assumption. Soto (1997) discusses why a model in which learning is substantial cannot be estimated using the standard, fixed-parameter model. In that case, the existence of an S-shaped learning curve would lead to substantially distorted and nonrobust results due to new information not reaching economic agents. A more sensible assumption would be to expect a learning curve, as FTZs evolve from infancy to maturity.

Taking this into consideration, the sources of growth analysis for the FTZs is carried out using a Kalman-filter specification:

$$\Delta Log_{Yt} = \alpha_0 \Delta Log_{Kt} + (1 - \alpha_0)\Delta Log_{Lt} + \qquad (3)$$
$$\beta[Log_{Yt-1} - \gamma - (\alpha_1 + SV_t) Log_{Kt-1} -$$
$$(1 - \alpha_1 - SV_t)Log_{Lt-1}] + \mu_t \text{ where } SV_t = \theta SV_{t-1} + vt$$

This specification allows parameters to evolve as agents learn to be more productive with given inputs. In standard microeconomic terms, the specification allows the FTZs to be initially at an interior point in the transformation curve and move sequentially towards the efficient frontier. A graphic display of the estimated time-evolving parameter is presented in Figure 4.

An analysis of the sources of growth for the FTZs (Table 22) shows remarkable productivity growth. From 1973 to 1998, the annual average productivity growth of the FTZs has consistently been more than four times higher than that of the rest of the economy. It must be pointed out, however, that because of data constraints, in recent years the estimate of total factor productivity growth has probably been overestimated, while capital accumulation, and therefore the contribution of capital to growth, has been underestimated. This result stems from the absence of detailed data on investment in the FTZs. Consequently, the area of their physical plants and their level of utilization is used as a proxy for capital. In recent years, however, as the constraints of market access to the United States have become more binding, there has been an important process of diversification that has

Figure 4. Kalman-Filter Estimates of the Share of Capital in FTZ Production Function

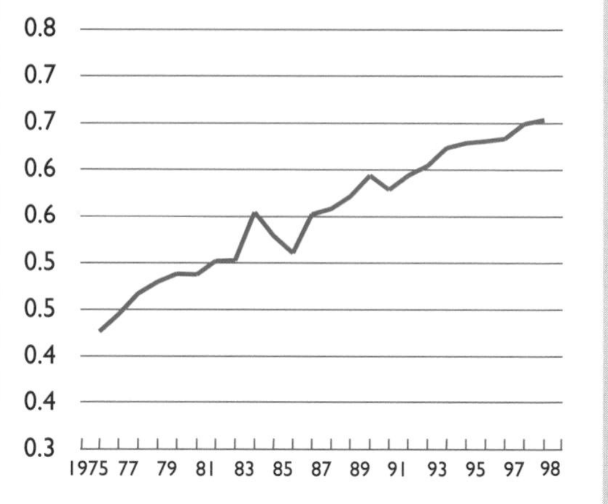

included increased vertical integration—and value added (VA)—in the production of garments, and also the development of other more capital-intensive products. Since these shifts can take place in the absence of expansion of the physical plants of the FTZs, total factor productivity growth is probably being overestimated.

Ultimately, however, whether because of different levels of investment and capital/labor ratios or because of differences in factor productivity growth, there is a clear difference in average productivity between the FTZs and the rest of the economy (Table 23). This important difference indicates the output gains that could be derived were the type of regulatory environment that applies to the FTZs to be extended to the economy at large.

The Role of Public Investment in Growth

The analysis in the preceding sections suggests that maintenance of strong growth in the Dominican Republic will hinge on at least three elements: maintaining macroeconomic stability; continuing to implement structural reforms that can help sustain high factor productivity growth; and increasing the rate of capital formation. In the past, the process of capital formation was reinforced by macroeconomic stability and the government's own public investment program. Since late 1996, however, there has been a significant shift in the composition of government expenditure, away from investment and toward cur-

Table 22. Estimates of Sources of Growth in the FTZs
(In percent)

Period	Value Added Growth (A year)	Capital Growth			Labor Growth			Total Factor Productivity Growth	
		Growth (A year)	Contribution to VA Growth	Share in VA Growth	Growth (A year)	Contribution to VA Growth	Share in VA Growth	Contribution to VA Growth	Share in VA Growth
1973–98	21.3	15.0	10.7	50.4	19.7	5.6	26.5	4.9	23.1
1973–82	18.9	11.7	8.4	44.4	25.0	7.1	37.9	3.3	17.8
1983–91	29.1	26.5	18.9	65.2	24.8	7.1	24.4	3.0	10.4
1992–98	14.7	4.9	3.5	23.8	5.6	1.6	10.9	9.6	65.4

Table 23. Average Productivity in the Economy and the FTZs
(In percent)

Period	Free-Trade Zones		Economy without FTZs	
	VA Growth	Growth in Average VA per Worker	GDP Growth	Growth in Average GDP per Worker
1973–98	21.3	3.28	4.6	1.12
1973–82	18.9	–2.23	5.6	2.10
1983–91	29.1	3.96	2.2	–1.56
1992–98	14.7	8.70	6.1	3.44

rent expenditure (including the wage bill) (Table 24). While some of the increase in the wage bill has been directed to finance human capital formation, this evolution raises concerns regarding its likely impact on private investment and, subsequently, on long-run growth.

To analyze the impact of the changing composition of public expenditures on growth and the ensuing policy implications, estimates were made of the *net* contribution of public investment to total investment.[65] There is a vast literature on modeling the determinants of investment based on the relation between output and the cost of capital (Jorgenson, 1971), the role of uncertainty (Abel, 1983), the response of investment to transitory output shocks (Blejer and Khan, 1984), and the role of the effect of real exchange rate changes on the profitability of investment projects and the cost of imported intermediate or capital goods (Krugman and Taylor, 1978). More recently, the role of economic stability has also been tested as a key determinant of private investment (Servén and Solimano, 1993). There is evidence that public investment may either crowd in or crowd out private investment, depending on the nature of those investments (Balassa, 1988; Khan and Reinhart, 1990; and Easterly, Rodríguez, and Schmidt-Hebbel, 1994). Estimates for the Dominican Republic are based on the following equation:

$$\frac{Priv.\ Inv_t}{GDP_t} = \tag{4}$$

$$f\left(\hat{GDP_t},\ Openness_t,\ \Delta Capital\ Cost_t, \right.$$

$$\left. W_t,\ \pi_t,\ \frac{Publ.\ Invt_t}{GDP_t},\ \frac{Gov.\ Const_t}{GDP_t} \right)$$

where openness is measure by the ratio of exports to GDP,[66] π is inflation, and W is the private real wage index.

The estimates presented in Table 25 show that in the Dominican Republic, public investment has had a net crowding-out effect on private investment since the parameter for total public investment is negative and significant, suggesting that for every percentage point of increased public investment,

[65]Some public investment can crowd out private investment, reducing its net contribution.

[66]Given past exchange controls and trade restrictions, the ratio of exports to GDP was seen as a better proxy for openness than the ratio of exports plus imports to GDP.

Table 24. Dominican Republic: Composition of Public Expenditures, 1995–98

(In percent of GDP)

	1995	1996	1997	1998
Current expenditures	7.2	7.8	10.6	11.1
Current expenditures adjusted[1]	6.0	6.5	9.1	n.a.
Wages	3.5	3.6	5.1	5.2
Transfers	1.9	2.5	3.3	3.5
Capital expenditures	7.0	6.6	5.5	5.1
Investment	4.5	4.6	2.8	2.7
Capital transfers	1.7	1.3	1.6	1.3
Amortization	0.7	0.7	1.6	0.8

Source: Based on information provided by ONAPRE.

[1]Current expenditures adjusted equals total current expenditures minus wages for education.

private investment decreases by 0.2 percentage point (Equation A). This crowding-out effect is significantly lower than that recently estimated by the World Bank (1998) for Mexico, where it reached a high 50 percent. Moreover, when separating the type of public investment between basic public goods and other nonpublic goods some interesting results and policy implications are obtained (Equation B). Public investment in basic public goods has a crowding-in effect of about 30 percent, thus contributing to *increased* private investment, while public investment in nonbasic public goods has a crowding-out effect of 15 percent. This would imply that even in the context of declining public investment the reallocation of public investments

towards core public goods would allow for continued strong capital formation.

Conclusion

The restoration of macroeconomic stability and the initiation of structural reforms in the early 1990s has led to strong economic growth and poverty reduction. Growth has been anchored by both a resurgence of capital formation and strong productivity growth, although the latter may be slightly overestimated given the imperfect measurement of human capital embodied in the measure of labor inputs.

With a ratio of investment to GDP of about 26 percent in 1998, high productivity growth and investment will be needed for a continuation of GDP growth rates of between 7 and 8 percent per year. The past performance of the Dominican Republic and international experience indicate that, in the absence of continued structural reforms, current rates of productivity growth will be hard to maintain. This implies that (1) the Dominican Republic should push forward with its implementation of structural reforms—recent developments are encouraging in this regard; and (2) strong capital formation needs to be maintained. To this end, increasing public investment *and* improving the focus of those investments to promote a crowding-in of private investment should be a priority.

Increases in real GDP growth rates and openness promote private investment. According to the empirical results, each extra percentage point of GDP in exports will raise private investment by 0.3 percentage point of GDP. Thus, the results are consistent with the notion that trade liberalization not only reduces price distortions and increases efficiency, but also encourages private investment and, ultimately, output growth.

Table 25. The Determinants of Private Investment, 1979–96

	Constant	Change Capital Cost	Lagged Change Wages	GDP Growth	Openness	Lagged Excess Capacity	Public Investment Total	Lagged Basic Public Goods[1]	Lagged Other[2]	AR(1)	R²	DW
Equation (A)	−2.353 (−10.47)	−0.013 (−1.59)	−0.234 (−1.72)	1.481 (3.70)	0.279 (2.36)	0.069 (3.09)	−0.177 (−2.50)		0.816 (9.84)	0.71	2.14	
Equation (B)	−1.258 (−2.92)	−0.019 (−2.37)	−0.129 (−1.32)	1.030 (4.41)	0.259 (2.39)	0.045 (1.14)		0.296 (3.88)	−0.151 (−2.98)	0.872 (8.51)	0.76	1.96

Source: World Bank estimates based on public investment classification from ONAPLAN. T-statistics are shown in parentheses.

[1]Basic public goods involve investments in transport, rural roads, water, and sewerage.

[2]Other includes housing, irrigation, communications, energy, agriculture, and urban developments.

Appendix V   Economy-Wide Data[*]

GDP is available in constant 1970 prices for the 1970–98 period.

The capital stock is estimated using the perpetual inventory method, assuming that the ratio of capital to GDP was 2½ in 1980, and the depreciation rate is 4 percent. Choosing a capital-output ratio in the range of 2½ to 3 is customary in TFP models (see for example, Pindyck, Servén, and Solimano, 1993; Sarel, 1997; and Braun and Braun, 1998). The selection of 1980 as a pivot for the estimation was based on the notion that excess capacity and macroeconomic imbalances were minimal at that time.

Employment data are not available for all periods, with a gap from 1984 to 1991. The gap was filled by estimating:

$$\text{Log Employment}_t = 6.76 + 0.035 \text{ Trend}_t + 0.458 \text{ Log Employment}_{t-1}$$
$$(139.2) \qquad (9.10) \qquad (2.69)$$
$$R^2 = 0.969$$

Breusch-Pagan Residual Correlation Test = 1.621

FTZ Data

Value added series in FTZs was obtained from the IMF for the 1983–98 period. For the 1970–82 period, total export figures were obtained from the study by Dauharje and others (1989), and it was assumed that value added was 30 percent of exports. This assumption is consistent with IMF data for the 1983–97 period, which estimates the ratio between 29 percent and 31 percent. Value added was deflated using the U.S. Producer Price Index to obtain real figures (valued in 1980 U.S. dollars).

The capital stock was proxied using data on physical investment (area of buildings) from the National Council of Free-Trade Zones. The latter is used for estimating the stock of capital with a perpetual inventory method under three assumptions: (1) the stock of capital in 1984 was US$238 million (Dauharje et al., 1989), (2) the average value of a square foot of con-

struction and equipment in FTZs was US$80.3 in 1984, including machinery (Dauhajre et al., 1989), and (3) depreciation rates were 4 percent per year.

Employment data are obtained directly from the National Council of Free-Trade Zones.

General Data Issues

The Dominican Republic has made significant advances in the quality of its national accounts data in the 1990s. Long-term data series, such as the ones used in this paper, may, however, suffer from certain limitations. Investment data for the late 1980s, a period of relatively high inflation and changing relative prices, may be subject to measurement problems. In this paper, the ratio of investment (I) to GDP was measured in real terms. However, measuring I/GDP in nominal terms yields different results. In the latter case, I/GDP remains fairly constant throughout the 1980s and 1990s, whereas I/GDP measured in real terms falls in the mid- to late-1980s, and rises in the 1990s. Thus, factor productivity growth is much higher in the 1990s when measuring I/GDP in real terms.

Unit Root Tests for Time Series Data

The series were first tested for unit roots (Table 28) using standard augmented Dickey-Fuller and Phillips-Perron tests (see Hamilton, 1994 for a description). Since the series are rather short—27 observations—tests were supplemented with the simple first-order autocorrelation of the series to classify series as integrated or trend stationary.

Estimates of the Production Function

Before estimating equations (2) and (3) (see main text) Granger causality tests were run between valued added and GDP and inputs. The results presented in Table 29 show that for the FTZs it is unlikely that there are simultaneity biases arising from the es-

---

[*]Data sources are described in Table 26. Data are shown in Table 27.

Table 26. Data Sources

Variables	Description	Source
National accounts	Official national accounts (base year 1970)	BCRD
Private and public investment	Breakdown of private and public investment	ONAPLAN
Price of capital goods	Ratio of investment deflator to GDP deflator	BCRD
Nominal exchange rate	Year average nominal exchange rate (in RD$ per U.S. dollar)	BCRD
CPI	Consumer price index, base year 1984	BCRD
Terms of trade	Terms of trade index	1965–92 Soto (1994)
		1993–97 World Bank
Wages	Real private wage index, base year 1984	1965–95 World Bank
		1996–97 Secretaría de Trabajo
Real exchange rate (RER)	Proxied by eP^*/CPI	P^* is the U.S. CPI index (base year 1984)
Capacity utilization	Potential GDP estimated using a nonlinear, quadratic model with intercept adjustments in 1980 along Clements and Hendry's (1999) methodology	Own calculation
r^*	International interest rate	U.S. 3-year t-bills, annualized
Openness	Exports in percent of GDP	BCRD
Value added in FTZ	Net exports	1970–82 Soto (1994), 1983–97 IMF
Labor in FTZ	Total employment	National Council of Free-Trade Zones
Capital in FTZ	Estimated using perpetual inventory (see text)	National Council of Free-Trade Zones

timation of the error-correction, cointegration models. Consequently, Engle-Granger estimation procedures can be undertaken without the disturbing presence of nuisance parameters. Estimates for the variables representing the non-FTZ economy show, however, that there is simultaneous causation between GDP and capital shocks. Simultaneity biases can be controlled, however, by including leads of capital shocks in the error-correction model, as discussed in Hargreaves (1994).

References

Abel, Andrew, 1983, "Optimal Investment under Uncertainty," *American Economic Review,* Vol. 73, pp. 228–33.

Balassa, Bela, 1988, "Public Finance and Economic Development," *PPR Working Paper No. 31,* The World Bank.

Blejer, Mario, and Mohsin Khan, 1984, "Government Policy and Private Investment in Developing Countries," *IMF Staff Papers,* Vol. 31.

Braun, J., and M. Braun, 1998, *El Crecimiento Potencial: El Caso de Chile,* mimeo, Pontificia Universidad Católica de Chile.

Clements, Michael P., and David F. Hendry, 1999, *Forecasting Non-Stationary Economic Time Series,* MIT Press, Boston, Mass.

Collins, Susan, Barry Bosworth, and Yu-chin Chen, 1996, "Accounting for Differences in Economic Growth," in Akira Kohsaka and Koichi Ohno (eds.). *Structural Adjustment and Economic Reform,* Tokyo, Japan: Institute of Developing Economics, 1996.

Dauharje, A., hijo, and others, 1989, *Impacto Económico de las Zonas Francas Industriales de Exportación en la República Dominicana,* Fundación Economía y Desarrollo.

Easterly, W., C.A. Rodríguez, and K. Schmidt-Hebbel, eds., 1994, *Public Sector Deficits and Macroeconomic Performance* (Oxford University Press for The World Bank).

Engle, R., and C. Granger, 1987, "Co-Integration and Error-Correction: Representation, Estimation, and Testing," *Econometrica,* Vol. 55, pp. 251–76.

Granger, C.W.J., 1969, "Investigating Causal Relations by Econometric Models and Cross-Spectral Models," *Econometrica,* Vol. 37, pp. 424–38.

———, and P. Newbold, 1974, "Spurious Regressions in Econometrics," *Journal of Econometrics,* Vol. 2, pp. 111–20.

Hamilton, J.D., 1994, *Time Series Analysis* (Princeton University Press, N.J.).

Table 27. Data Used in Estimations and Simulations

	Free-Trade Zones			Economy (Except FTZs)				
Year	Value Added (In millions of 1984 U.S. dollars)	Capital Stock (In thousands of 1984 U.S. dollars)	Employment (In thousands)	GDP (In millions of 1970 pesos)	Capital Stock (In millions of 1970 pesos)	Employment (In thousands)	Private Investment (In millions of 1970 pesos)	Public Investment (In millions of 1970 pesos)
1970	4.0	8.0	0.5	1,485.5	4,682.8	1,030.5	208.0	76.3
1971	8.0	21.0	1.0	1,647.0	4,779.4	1,080.0	227.5	105.7
1972	12.7	32.2	2.3	1,818.2	4,882.7	1,022.0	259.6	115.1
1973	12.4	55.3	3.2	2,052.8	5,046.1	1,202.0	342.8	132.7
1974	19.3	68.1	4.8	2,176.0	5,297.8	1,230.6	382.2	151.0
1975	26.5	81.1	7.0	2,288.9	5,598.2	1,234.2	426.1	186.0
1976	33.6	94.5	8.6	2,442.9	5,935.3	1,348.7	430.9	141.8
1977	42.9	98.7	10.9	2,564.5	6,242.4	1,391.0	486.9	132.0
1978	49.3	100.1	13.5	2,619.6	6,611.6	1,397.5	516.5	119.1
1979	53.6	92.5	16.1	2,738.2	6,982.8	1,434.4	553.6	133.9
1980	52.2	83.9	18.3	2,956.4	7,391.0	1,414.6	603.6	144.4
1981	62.0	81.1	20.5	3,082.9	7,843.4	1,497.6	543.7	123.8
1982	64.4	83.5	19.6	3,135.3	8,197.1	1,508.1	470.4	77.6
1983	120.5	92.7	22.3	3,280.4	8,417.2	1,601.7	495.7	99.1
1984	99.1	118.4	27.1	3,321.5	8,675.3	1,598.7	548.3	74.5
1985	85.2	156.4	35.7	3,251.0	8,951.0	1,735.5	494.0	99.5
1986	174.2	270.9	51.2	3,365.5	9,186.5	1,783.6	485.1	132.1
1987	188.2	295.7	66.0	3,706.0	9,436.2	1,834.6	653.7	291.3
1988	239.8	360.6	83.8	3,785.9	10,003.8	1,885.0	429.4	374.1
1989	336.2	424.3	122.9	3,952.5	10,407.1	1,916.5	604.2	342.3
1990	332.5	586.7	130.0	3,736.9	10,937.4	1,982.6	572.8	223.1
1991	423.0	630.8	135.5	3,773.2	11,295.8	2,116.2	525.9	200.6
1992	514.4	706.2	141.1	4,075.7	11,570.4	2,265.3	634.3	265.6
1993	665.1	725.6	164.3	4,198.6	12,005.6	2,252.4	623.9	342.1
1994	704.5	733.1	176.3	4,380.7	12,593.3	2,224.3	649.7	376.6
1995	761.9	774.2	165.6	4,591.4	13,162.1	2,235.1	847.9	300.6
1996	793.4	762.8	164.6	4,925.0	13,755.0	2,358.4	914.6	331.6
1997	974.7	780.0	182.2	5,326.4	14,430.4	2,469.8	1,055.5	244.8
1998	1,080.8	877.0	195.2	5,712.9	15,310.1	2,530.5	...	...

Hargreaves, C., 1994, "A Review of Methods of Estimating Cointegrating Relationships" in *Non Stationary Time Series Analysis and Cointegration* (Oxford University Press).

Jorgenson, Dale, 1971, "Econometric Studies of Investment Behavior: A Survey," *Journal of Economic Literature,* Vol. 9, pp. 1111–47.

Khan, Mohsin S., and C.M. Reinhart, 1990, "Private Investment and Economic Growth in Developing Countries," *World Development,* Vol. 18, No. 1.

Krugman, Paul, and Lance Taylor, 1978, "The Contractionary Effects of Devaluations," *Journal of International Economics,* Vol. 8, pp. 445–56.

Maddison, August, 1987, "Growth and Slowdowns in Advanced Capitalist Economies: Techniques of Qualitative Assessments," *Journal of Economic Literature,* Vol. 25, pp. 649–98.

Pindyck, R., 1993, "Irreversibility, Uncertainty, and Investment," *Striving for Growth After Adjustment: The Role of Capital Formation,* L. Servén and A. Solimano (eds.). The World Bank.

Sarel, Michael, 1997, "Growth and Productivity in ASEAN Countries," IMF Working Paper 97/97.

Senhadji, Abdelhak, 1999, "Sources of Economic Growth: An Extensive Growth Accounting Exercise," IMF Working Paper 99/77.

Servén, Luis, and Andrés Solimano, 1993, "Private Investment and Macroeconomic Adjustment: A Survey"; *Striving for Growth After Adjustment. The Role of Capital Formation,* L. Servén and A. Solimano (eds.). The World Bank.

Solow, Robert M., 1956, "A Contribution to the Theory of Economic Growth," *Quarterly Journal of Economics,* Vol. 70, pp. 65–94.

Table 28. Unit Root Tests

	First Order Autocorrelation	Variable in Levels		ADF First Difference
		ADF*	PP*	
Value added in FTZ	0.858	−1.55	−2.08	−5.94
Capital stock in FTZ	0.831	−0.80	−2.40	−2.80
Employment in FTZ	0.855	−2.11	−3.12	−4.24
GDP rest of economy (ROE)	0.887	−2.44	−2.89	−3.90
Capital stock ROE	0.928	−2.61	−3.22	−2.84
Employment in ROE	0.916	−1.04	−1.32	−3.43
Private investment (in percent of GDP)	0.577	−3.67	−3.69	. . .
Public investment (in percent of GDP)	0.696	−2.87	−2.99	
Terms of trade	0.377	−3.53	−3.86	. . .
Real exchange rate	0.538	−2.97	−3.01	. . .
Real wages	0.746	−2.20	−2.16	−5.49
Alternative cost of capital	0.780	−1.34	−1.20	−4.78
Relative cost of capital goods	0.418	−4.12	−3.12	. . .
Inflation	0.365	−3.79	−3.81	. . .
TFP growth ROE	0.176	−4.12	−4.08	. . .
Openness	0.675	−2.11	−2.08	−5.98
Capacity utilization	0.169	−5.18	−4.68	. . .
Public investment in infrastructure	0.707	−2.48	−3.09	. . .
Public investment in social capital	0.772	−4.09**	. . .	. . .
Public investment in housing and urban development	0.863	−3.00**	. . .	. . .

Note: (*) ADF is the augmented Dickey-Fuller Test and PP is Phillips-Perron unit root test. Critical value is −2.62 at 90 percent. (**) The Perron structural break test was performed, allowing for a jump in the mean of the series in 1984.

Table 29. Causality Tests

Test	F-Test	Test	F-Test
GDP does not Granger cause employment	1.5	Value added does not Granger cause employment	1.07
Employment does not Granger cause GDP	2.92*	Employment does not Granger cause value added	3.02*
GDP does not Granger cause capital	3.25*	Value added does not Granger cause capital	0.36
Capital does not Granger cause GDP	5.23*	Capital does not Granger cause value added	0.35

Soto, R., 1994, "A Macroeconomic Assessment of the Dominican Republic: Policies and Prospects," mimeo, The World Bank.

———, 1997, "Non-Linearities in the Demand for Money: A Neural Network Approach," Working Paper Series No.107, ILADES-Georgetown University.

World Bank, 1998, Mexico: Country Economic Assessment, mimeo.

VI Money Demand in a Small Open Economy: The Case of the Dominican Republic

The formulation of monetary policy in the Dominican Republic is centered around an annual monetary program prepared by the BCRD and discussed with the government.[67] The theoretical framework of the program is the monetary approach to the balance of payments. Given expected annual real output growth, together with the inflation and exchange rate/foreign reserve objectives of the monetary authorities, an estimated money demand establishes a constraint on the assets and liabilities of the BCRD's balance sheet. The program also specifies quarterly objectives for the intermediate targets (currency) and monetary policy instruments (for example, central bank paper). The quarterly objectives serve as guidelines for the Monetary and Exchange Affairs Committee as it monitors higher frequency indicators of the demand for money. Deviations from the projected path trigger a consultation with the governor of the BCRD and the Monetary Board, which ultimately decides which course of action to take.

The main instrument used for the implementation of monetary policy is central bank paper called *certificados de participación*. However, the BCRD also manages liquidity in the system using direct measures such as credit controls and the occasional freezing of excess reserves held at the BCRD by financial institutions. The BCRD intervenes in the free (commercial bank) foreign exchange market mostly with the objective of smoothing the irregular and seasonal components of exchange rate behavior, relinquishing in those cases the control of monetary aggregates.[68] Since late 1991, interest rates have been freely determined by market forces.

The objective of this chapter is to estimate a money demand equation for the Dominican Repub-lic. The motivation is threefold. The key role that money demand plays in the formulation and implementation of monetary policy in the Dominican Republic contrasts with the doubt, both in academia and among policymakers (Leiderman and Svensson, 1995; and Blinder, 1998), that there is a long-run relationship (cointegration) between real money aggregates and real income.[69] The first motivation for estimating a money demand equation for the Dominican Republic is thus to test whether there is a long-run (cointegrating) relationship between real monetary aggregates, real income, and interest rates.

The second motivation for this study is to have a more informed view on the ability of the BCRD to control money market conditions and insulate them from foreign influences. Since the seminal work by Mundell (1963) on capital mobility and stabilization policy under fixed and flexible exchange rates, it has been recognized that the ability of monetary authorities in a small open economy to set monetary conditions, independent of foreign factors, decreases as capital mobility increases.[70] In a small open economy with capital mobility, a policy-induced increase in interest rates encourages capital inflows, which eliminate the incipient change in the interest rate differential and appreciate the domestic currency. In the Dominican Republic, as the domestic financial market and the capital account were liberalized, and as the economy started an extended period of high growth, monetary policy experienced a growing difficulty in maintaining a desired interest rate differential. The exchange rate effects stemming from changes in the domestic interest rate have been countered by foreign exchange market intervention, which has not always been fully sterilized. As a result, the stock of *certificados de participación* has increased over time, and the growth of monetary ag-

---

[67]The Monetary and Financial Code currently being discussed in congress would require that the monetary program be submitted to congress.

[68]There is a dual foreign exchange market in the Dominican Republic: all traditional exports, credit card, and telecommunication transactions are subject to surrender requirements (about 15 percent of the total volume of foreign exchange transactions) and the remainder goes through the free market. The BCRD is responsible for providing foreign exchange for the payment of the country's petroleum import bill and the servicing of the public sector's foreign debt.

[69]This has been the main practical factor behind the move in industrialized countries away from controlling monetary aggregates and toward controlling interest rates.

[70]In the extreme case of perfect capital mobility (that is, when domestic and foreign securities are perfect substitutes and financial markets are efficient), monetary policy cannot make the differential between domestic and foreign real interest rates different from zero.

gregates has been endogenized.[71] This is not the end of the story, however. As those capital inflows are intermediated by the banking system, they have resulted in a relatively higher rate of credit growth and have put downward pressure on interest rates. The main point is that the final effect of the original monetary policy tightening on overall monetary conditions seems to have been smaller than its initial effect, both on M2 and on the interest rate. Appendix VI.1 develops an open economy model to illustrate this point.

The third motivation, a corollary of the last point, is to relate the issue of the ability of the BCRD to control domestic monetary conditions independently of foreign influences to the recent debate on how to assess the stance of monetary policy (see Christiano and others, 1998). The literature normally finds that a contractionary monetary policy increases domestic interest rates and appreciates the domestic currency. This highlights the role of capital flows in open economies discussed above. This was at the heart of much debate on the recent Asian crisis. The press has argued that high interest rates in Asia indicated a "tight" monetary policy. Based on the growth of monetary aggregates, Corsetti and others (1998) have characterized the monetary policy stance in Asia as "loose." This debate suggests that the "monetary policy stance" may not be well measured by interest rates alone, or by the growth of monetary aggregates alone, whenever there is rapid feedback between monetary aggregates, credit, and interest rates, as is the case in small open economies. Interest rates contain both policy- and market-determined elements, and it is important to consider the evolution over time of financial variables in accurately assessing the stance of monetary policy (Tanner, 1999).

Econometric estimators of money demand equations should be able to deal with the suggested endogeneity of interest rates. This paper uses a Phillips-Loretan (1991) nonlinear dynamic least squares estimator to estimate three versions of a money demand equation—one that uses as a regressor a domestic interest rate, another one that uses the interest rate differential between the Dominican Republic and the United States, and a third one that uses the U.S. interest rate.

The Estimated Equations and the Estimation Technique

Given the theoretical framework of the Dominican Republic's monetary program, this paper uses two measures of real monetary aggregates, M1 and M2, and investigates whether they are cointegrated with real output and nominal interest rates. Different specifications of equation (A7) in Appendix VI.1 are estimated.[72] The basic money demand equation (A7), with all variables except interest rates expressed in logs, is repeated here for convenience:

$$\left(\frac{M}{P}\right)_t = b_0 + b_1 y_t + b_2 i_t + \varepsilon_t^{m^d} \qquad (1)$$

The coefficients in equation (1) have the standard interpretation seen in studies of money demand dynamics: b_1 measures the output elasticity of money while b_2 measures the semielasticity of substitution between money and other domestic assets (that is, financial and real assets). It should be noted that the only interest-bearing financial assets readily available in the Dominican Republic are savings and time deposits, which are part of M2 but not M1. As a result, in the case of M2, b_2 is to be interpreted as the semielasticity of substitution between money and domestic real assets.

Because the Dominican Republic is a small economy with no capital controls, given uncovered interest rate parity (equation A8), equation (1) becomes:

$$\left(\frac{M}{P}\right)_t = b_0 + b_1 y_t + b_2[i_t^* + (E_t e_{t+1} - e_t)] + \varepsilon_t^{m^d} \qquad (2)$$

The constant term in (2) now also includes a constant country risk premium. As before, the third term in equation (2) measures the semielasticity of substitution between money and other domestic assets. However, in an open economy, capital mobility equalizes the risk-adjusted expected return on domestic and foreign interest-bearing assets. So, in an open economy, the third term measures as well the degree of substitutability between domestic and foreign interest-bearing assets. This term poses special econometric problems because the expected change in the exchange rate is unobservable. The expected exchange rate change could be proxied by the difference between the forward and spot rates. Unfortunately, there is no forward market in the Dominican Republic, and as a result, equation (2) cannot be estimated in that form. Thus, given the objective of assessing the capacity of monetary policy to control domestic monetary conditions in isolation of foreign influences, one can use the coefficient on the interest rate differential $(i_t - i_t^*)$ as a proxy for the degree of substitutability between domestic and foreign interest-bearing assets. This follows a long tradition in money demand estimation in open economies (for example, Cuddington, 1983, and Siklos, 1996). The equation to estimate is:

$$\left(\frac{M}{P}\right)_t = b_0 + b_1 y_t + b_2(i - i^*)_t + \varepsilon_t^{m^d} \qquad (3)$$

---

[71]The measure of M2 used in this study includes foreign currency–denominated deposits.

[72]The variables are defined in Appendix VI.1.

As stated above, the estimate of b_2 from equation (2) measures either the semielasticity of substitution between money and domestic interest-bearing assets or the semielasticity of substitution between domestic and foreign interest-bearing assets. If the latter coefficient is statistically equal to the estimate of b_2 from equation (1)—which only measures the semielasticity of substitution between money and domestic interest-bearing assets—it is still possible to argue that the variance in the interest rate differential in equation (3) is driven mostly by the variance of the domestic interest rate. In that case, one could conclude that the home country monetary authorities can largely control domestic money market conditions independently of foreign influences, and that capital mobility is low. Therefore, for testing that hypothesis, as well as for completeness, a version of a money demand equation that uses the foreign interest rate is also estimated:[73]

$$\left(\frac{M}{P}\right)_t = b_0 + b_1 y_t + b_2 i_t^* + \varepsilon_t^{md} \qquad (4)$$

If there is a long-run relationship among real monetary aggregates, real output, and interest rates, there will be feedback between that long-run equilibrium relationship and the errors that drive the regressors (that is, real output and interest rates). Ordinary least squares (OLS), single equation error correction methods, and unrestricted vector autoregressions (VAR) will lead to estimators that are asymptotically biased and inefficient.[74] Therefore, equations (1), (3), and (4) are estimated using the nonlinear dynamic least squares estimator of Phillips and Loretan (1991). The authors show that this single-equation technique is asymptotically equivalent to a maximum likelihood estimator on a full system of equations under Gaussian assumptions. The technique provides estimators that are statistically efficient, and whose t-ratios can be used for inference in the usual way. Most importantly, the method takes into account both the serial correlation of the errors and the endogeneity of the regressors that are present when there is a cointegration relationship. The three estimated specifications are represented by equations (5)–(7),

$$\left(\frac{M}{P}\right)_t = a + by_t + ci_t + \sum_{j=-k}^{k}[d_j\Delta y_{t-j} + e_j\Delta i_{t-j}] + \qquad (5)$$

$$\rho[\left(\frac{M}{P}\right)_{t-1} - a - by_{t-1} - ci_{t-1}] + \varepsilon_t$$

$$\left(\frac{M}{P}\right)_t = a + by_t + c(i - i^*)_t + \sum_{j=-k}^{k}[d_j\Delta y_{t-j} + \qquad (6)$$

$$e_j\Delta(i - i^*)_{t-j}] + \rho[\left(\frac{M}{P}\right)_{t-1} - a - by_{t-1} - c(i - i^*)_{t-1}] + \eta_t$$

$$\left(\frac{M}{P}\right)_t = a + by_t + ci^*_t + \sum_{j=-k}^{k}[d_j\Delta y_{t-j} + e_j\Delta i^*_{t-j}] + \qquad (7)$$

$$\rho[\left(\frac{M}{P}\right)_{t-1} - a - by_{t-1} - ci_t^*] + \xi_t$$

Note that equations (5)–(7) include leads and not just lags. Phillips and Loretan, 1991, show that leads are required to produce valid conditioning (that is, to make the residuals ε_t, η_t, and ξ_t orthogonal to the entire history of the regressors). Similarly, the estimator includes not only lagged changes in the left-hand side variable $\left(\frac{M}{P}\right)_{t-1}$ but also the lagged equilibrium relationship. The reason is that lags of $\left(\frac{M}{P}\right)_{t-1}$ are not good good proxies for the past history of ε_t, η_t, and ξ_t because of the persistence in effects of innovations from the unit roots in equations (1), (3), and (4). This requires the use of a nonlinear technique.

The standard interpretation of the coefficients b_1 and b_2 in equations (1), (3), and (4) was discussed above. That interpretation referred to the short-run dynamics of money demand, and it is also applicable to the coefficients d_j and e_j in equations (5)–(7). However, equations (5)–(7) require the interpretation of the long-run values of the coefficients b and c as well. Those long-run values constitute the main focus of this study because they are the parameter estimates of the *long-run* relationship between money aggregates, real output, and interest rates. It is expected that $b = 1$ for both M1 and M2 (at least when the interest rates used are the domestic interest rate or the interest rate differential). In the case of M1, it is expected that $c < 0$ because holding noninterest bearing money is costly. However, it is also possible that M1 is held in the long run only for transaction purposes, in which case $c = 0$. As indicated earlier, because M2 includes foreign currency-denominated deposits, and given the frequent foreign exchange interventions of the BCRD, the long-run correlation between real M2 and the domestic interest rate or the interest rate differential may be positive, suggesting that $c > 0$. Similarly, in the relatively underdeveloped Dominican financial markets, time deposits (quasi-money) serve as the main savings assets instrument, also suggesting that $c > 0$ for M2.[75] Because i^* proxies the rate of

---

[73]Another specification, where both the domestic and the foreign interest rates enter the regression separately, was estimated. Results are available upon request.

[74]See Goldfeld and Sichel's (1990) survey on the empirical difficulties and the econometric issues dealt with in the money demand estimation literature. See also Laidler (1994).

[75]Alternatively, it has been suggested that the long-run coefficient c reflects money's own rate of return and it is therefore expected to be positively correlated with M2.

Table 30. Dominican Republic: Unit Root Tests at 5 Percent Level
(1992:Q1–1999:Q1)

$$\Delta X_t = \alpha + \beta_t + \gamma X_{t-1} + \sum_{i=1}^{p-1} \phi i \Delta X_{t-i} + \varepsilon_t$$

Variable	Lags[1]	Dickey-Fuller				Phillips-Perron			
		$T_\mu{}^2$	$T_\tau{}^2$	$\rho_\mu{}^3$	$\rho_\tau{}^3$	$T_\mu{}^2$	$T_\tau{}^2$	$\rho_\mu{}^3$	$\rho_\tau{}^3$
M1	2	−1.37	−3.66*	−2.62	−85.99*	−0.75	−2.27	−1.06	−10.35
M2	3	−0.10	−3.26	−0.14	154.84	−0.34	−2.02	−0.34	−8.68
GDP	5	−4.11*	−4.30*	−0.83	−2.64	−7.12*	−14.19*	−4.01	−8.29
IDOM	1	−2.53	−2.46	−16.72*	−16.78	−1.86	−1.81	−7.77	−7.55
IRD	1	−1.94	−1.89	−9.93	−11.55	−1.63	−1.38	−5.93	−5.32
MID	3	−3.93*	−3.81*	55.66	55.46	−3.54*	−3.50	−18.26*	−18.11
M2D	3	−3.68*	−3.69*	151.63	429.76	−3.30*	−3.23	−18.15*	−18.09
GDPD	6	−1.50	−2.70	−1.86	−6.67	−15.52*	−12.42*	−5.40	−5.83
IDOMD	1	−3.13*	−3.40	−19.73*	−22.17*	−3.78*	−3.97*	−16.88*	−17.14
IRDD	1	−3.13*	−3.77*	−18.66*	−23.12*	−4.17*	−4.66*	−17.82*	−18.22*
Probability of a smaller value 5 percent		−2.99	−3.58	−12.63	−18.20	−2.99	−3.58	−12.63	−18.20

Sources: BCRD; and IMF staff estimates.
Note: IDOM = 90-day lending rate in the Dominican Republic.
   IRD = interest rate differential; that is, 90-day lending rate in the Dominican Republic minus 90-day T-bill rate in the United States.
   M1D = M1 first differenced.
   M2D = M2 first differenced.
   GDPD = GDP first differenced.
   IDOMD = 90-day lending rate in the Dominican Republic first differenced.
   IRDD = 90-day lending rate in the Dominican Republic minus 90-day T-bill rate in the United States first differenced.
   [1]Lags were chosen according to the Akaike Information Criterion and for white noise of the residuals.
   [2]The power of ρ_μ (only constant) and ρ_τ (constant and time trend) is higher than the power of T_μ (only constant) and T_τ (constant and time trend) when the alternative is stationary.
   [3]The Newey-West weighting scheme was used for estimating the variances of $S_\mu{}^2$ and $S_\tau{}^2$.

return on foreign assets, given an expected change in the exchange rate, the correlation between either real M1 or real M2 and the foreign interest rate is expected to be negative.

Equations (5)–(7) were estimated using quarterly data from 1992:Q1 to 1999:Q1. There are no indices of real activity available at a higher frequency in the Dominican Republic. Extending the sample back in time would imply going into a period when interest rates were not market-determined and important structural reforms had not yet taken place. The domestic interest rate used was the 90-day deposit rate and the foreign interest rate used was the 90-day U.S. treasury bill rate.

Unit Roots, Cointegration, and Long-Run Elasticities

Tables 30 and 31 report the results for unit root tests.[76] In general, the tests tend to indicate that real

---

[76]See Appendix VI.2 for a detailed description of the unit root and cointegration tests performed.

M1, real M2, the domestic interest rate, and the interest rate differential are unit root processes. In the case of real output, however, only one of the two tests accepted the unit root hypothesis, but it was the more powerful of the two. Other econometric tests were also consistent with a unit root in real output. The behavior of the foreign interest rate during the sample period suggested that the unit root test should have power with respect to an alternative which allows for possible breaks either in the intercept or in the slope of the series. The Perron (1997) test did not reject the unit root hypothesis.

Tests for cointegration were based on the Johansen-Juselius (1990) method with critical values corrected for small sample bias using Cheung and Lai's (1993) approach (Table 32).

Tests of the residuals indicated that they were not serially correlated. Overall, there is strong statistical evidence of a long-run cointegration relationship between real monetary aggregates, real output, and interest rates in the Dominican Republic during the sample period. For more information on the tests also see Appendix VI.2.

Table 31. Perron (1997) Unit Root Test on the Foreign Interest Rate at 5 Percent[1]
(1992:Q1–1999:Q1)

Model 1:
$$y_t = u + \Theta DU_t + \beta_t + \delta D(T_b)_t + \alpha y_{t-1} + \sum_{i=1}^{k} c_i \Delta y_{t-i} + e_t$$

$T_b{}^2$	k^3	$\hat{\alpha}$	$\hat{t}_\alpha$	$\hat{t}_\theta$
1995:3	10	0.62	6.09	n.a.
1996:2	10	1.24	n.a.	8.45

Model 2:
$$y_t = u + \Theta DU_t + \beta_t + \delta DT_t + \delta D(T_b)_t + \alpha y_{t-1} + \sum_{i=1}^{k} c_i \Delta y_{t-i} + e_t$$

$T_b{}^2$	k^3	$\hat{\alpha}$	$\hat{t}_\alpha$	$\hat{t}_\theta$
1997:1	8	−3.20	−5.36	n.a.
1997:1	8	−3.20	n.a.	−5.36

[1]The critical values used correspond to 60 observations tabulated in Perron (1997).

[2]T_b is the value that minimizes the t-statistic for testing $\alpha = 1$.

[3]The k maximum was selected using the general to specific recursive procedure.

The Long-Run Elasticities of the Model

Although the main objective of this paper is to test the existence of a long-run relationship between real monetary aggregates, real output, and interest rates, it was also thought important to look into the dynamics of the short-run disequilibrium. As a result, Table 33 reports not only the long-run parameters of the models, but also the parameters of the short-run dynamics from the Phillips-Loretan nonlinear dynamic least squares estimator.[77]

Analysis of the residuals indicated that they were white noise; there is agreement between the nonparametric test (Bartlett-Kolmogorov-Smirnov) at the 10 percent level and the visual observation of the resid-

[77]The tests were started using a lag (and lead) structure similar to that in Johansen-Juselius (1990). The lag-lead structure necessary to eliminate serial correlation varied across models; one lag and one lead were preferred for all cases except for real M2 and the domestic interest rate where two leads and two lags were preferred. Similarly, for real M1 and the foreign interest rate two lags and one lead were preferred. In all cases, however, conscious about Phillips and Loretan's warning of over-fitting, the number of leads was reduced by one first. Lags were reduced then if necessary. The parameter estimates and their significance, as well as whether the residuals were white noise, were checked every time.

[78]Figures 5–10 have an upper and a lower confidence interval calculated as a Bartlett's test that is normally distributed. The confidence intervals are wide due to the relatively short sample period. However, note that 100 observations would give a value of ±0.20 for the 95 percent level and about ±0.16 for the 90 percent level. The residuals are well within those bands.

uals in Figures 5–10.[78] The residuals are also homoscedastic according to two chi-square tests using one and four lags.[79]

The constant and the long-run output elasticity are significant at the 99 percent level. As expected, the long-run output elasticity is not statistically different from one in equations (5) and (6) at the 90 percent level (and above) as denoted by the χ^2 statistic. The long-run output elasticity is different from one only when the foreign interest rate is used in the regression.

The long-run interest rate semielasticity of real M1 is not statistically different from zero at conventional confidence levels. A possible rationalization of this result requires appealing to the steady state of the model of Appendix VI.1, solved in Nadal-De Simone (2001). In the long run (steady state), the rate of

[79]The R^2 is reported although in a cointegrated system, estimated with valid conditioning, the R^2 is not meaningful as a measure of fit.

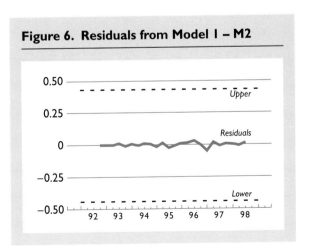

Figure 5. Residuals from Model 1 – M1

Figure 6. Residuals from Model 1 – M2

Table 32. The Johansen-Juselius Maximum Likelihood Test for Cointegration
(1992:Q1–1999:Q1)

	Eigen Values	λ max	Trace	H₀: r	p-r	λ max 95%	λ max 99%	Trace 95%	Trace 99%	Lags
M1-inter. Rate	0.8517	51.53*	68.09*	0	3	17.69	19.13	37.01	43.94	2
	0.4582	16.55*	16.56	1	2	14.48	16.45	19.32	24.81	
	0.0003	0.01	0.01	2	1	4.84	8.36	4.84	8.36	
Residuals										
Normality ∼χ₆² = 6.038 (0.42)			LM1 ∼χ₉² = 14.793 (0.10)					LM4 ∼χ₉² = 8.923 (0.44)		
M2-inter. Rate	0.8048	44.12*	63.50*	0	3	17.69	19.13	37.01	43.94	2
	0.5069	19.09*	19.38**	1	2	14.48	16.45	19.32	24.81	
	0.0108	0.29	0.29	2	1	4.84	8.36	4.84	8.36	
Residuals										
Normality ∼χ₆² = 11.187 (0.08)			LM1 ∼χ₉² = 25.675 (0.00)					LM4 ∼χ₉² = 13.593 (0.14)		
M1-inter. diff.	0.8873	58.94*	73.95*	0	3	17.69	19.13	37.01	43.94	2
	0.4254	14.96**	15.01	1	2	14.48	16.45	19.32	24.81	
	0.0019	0.05	0.05	2.	1.	4.84	8.36	4.84	8.36	
Residuals										
Normality ∼χ₆² = 3.693 (0.72)			LM1 ∼χ₉² = 15.643 (0.07)					LM4 ∼χ₉² = 9.600 (0.38)		
M2-inter. diff.	0.8578	52.67*	72.44*	0	3	17.69	19.13	37.01	43.94	2
	0.5175	19.68**	19.77**	1	2	14.48	16.45	19.32	24.81	
	0.0036	0.10	0.10	2	1	4.84	8.36	4.84	8.36	
Residuals										
Normality ∼χ₆² = 6.731 (0.35)			LM1 ∼χ₉² = 23.128 (0.01)					LM4 ∼χ₉² = 15.882 (0.07)		
M1-foreign inter. rate	0.9026	62.89*	76.89*	0	3	17.69	19.13	37.01	43.94	
	0.3182	10.34	14.00	1	2	14.49	16.45	19.32	24.81	2
	0.1268	3.66	3.66	2	1	4.84	8.36	4.84	8.36	
Residuals										
Normality ∼χ₆² = 7.949 (0.24)			LM1 ∼χ₉² = 19.747 (0.02)					LM4 ∼χ₉² = 12.465 (0.19)		
M2-foreign inter. rate	0.7960	42.92*	61.54*	0	3	17.69	19.13	37.01	43.94	
	0.4547	16.37**	18.61	1	2	14.49	16.45	19.32	24.81	2
	0.0797	2.24	2.24	2	1	4.84	8.36	4.84	8.36	
Residuals										
Normality ∼χ₆² = 9.865 (0.13)			LM1 ∼χ₉² = 9.716 (0.37)					LM4 ∼χ₉² = 13.976 (0.12)		

Sources: BCRD; and IMF staff estimates.

r is the number of cointegrated vectors.

p is the number of variables.

The 99 percent (denoted with *) and 95 percent (denoted with **) critical values corrected for small samples using Cheung and Lai (1993) are used to evaluate the results.

The models include a drift term in the variables but not in the cointegration space. The normality test is a multivariate version of the Shenton-Bowman test for normality for individual time series. The LM1 and LM4 are the Langrange multiplier tests. p values are in parentheses.

Table 33. The Phillips-Loretan Nonlinear Dynamic Least Squares Estimator
(1992–99:Q1)

$$\text{Equation 5:} \left(\frac{M}{P}\right)_t = a + by_t + ci_t + \sum_{j=-k}^{k}(d_j\Delta y_{t-j} + e_j\Delta i_{t-j}) + \rho\left[\left(\frac{M}{P}\right)_{t-1} - a - by_{t-1} - ci_{t-1}\right] + \varepsilon_t$$

	M1			M2	
Constant	−4.87	(−2.68)	Constant	−7.09	(−3.29)
y_t	0.73	(4.50)	y_t	0.95	(4.65)
i_i	0.02	(0.65)	i_i	0.05	(2.17)
Δy_{t-1}	−0.27	(−2.76)	Δy_{t-2}	−0.63	(−1.79)
Δi_{t-1}	−0.02	(−5.06)	Δi_{t-2}	−0.01	(−0.86)
Δy_t	0.30	(0.78)	Δy_{t-1}	0.28	(0.77)
Δi_t	−0.03	(−1.06)	Δi_{t-1}	−0.02	(−3.63)
Δy_{t+1}	0.24	(0.64)	Δy_t	0.00	(0.00)
Δi_{t+1}	−0.00	(−1.08)	Δi_t	−0.04	(−1.94)
ρ	−0.83	(−11.98)	Δy_{t+1}	1.58	(1.46)
			Δi_{t+1}	0.00	(0.03)
			Δy_{t+2}	2.05	(2.76)
			Δi_{t+2}	0.01	(1.29)
			ρ	−0.68	(−4.56)

$\bar{R}^2 = 0.98$	SE = 0.02	$\bar{R}^2 = 0.98$	SE = 0.02
$\chi^2_1 = 0.04$	$\chi^2_4 = 1.58$	$\chi^2_1 = 0.05$	$\chi^2_4 = 1.21$
B-K-S = 0.27	b = 1 ~ $\chi^2_1 = 2.75$	B-K-S = 0.22	b = 1 ~ $\chi^2_1 = 0.05$

$$\text{Equation 6:} \left(\frac{M}{P}\right)_t = a + by_t + c(i - i^*)_t + \sum_{j=-k}^{k}[d_j\Delta y_{t-j} + e_j\Delta(i - i^*)_{t-j}] + \rho\left[\left(\frac{M}{P}\right)_{t-1} - a - by_{t-1} - c(i - i^*)_{t-1}\right] + \eta_t$$

Constant	−6.01	(−3.28)	Constant	−4.41	(−2.29)
y_t	0.84	(4.87)	y_t	0.75	(4.29)
$(i - i^*)_t$	0.02	(1.36)	$(i - i^*)_t$	0.06	(2.48)
Δy_{t-1}	−0.26	(−2.40)	Δy_{t-1}	−0.22	(−2.25)
Δi_{t-1}	−0.02	(−4.98)	Δi_{t-1}	−0.02	(−4.08)
Δy_t	0.41	(1.13)	Δy_t	0.39	(1.04)
$\Delta(i - i^*)_t$	−0.03	(−2.20)	$\Delta(i - i^*)_t$	−0.06	(−2.54)
Δy_{t+1}	0.47	(1.26)	Δy_{t+1}	0.04	(0.08)
$\Delta(i - i^*)_{t+1}$	−0.01	(−1.54)	$\Delta(i - i^*)_{t+1}$	0.00	(0.20)
ρ	−0.79	(−11.99)	ρ	−0.80	(−13.59)

$\bar{R}^2 = 0.98$	SE = 0.02	$\bar{R}^2 = 0.98$	SE = 0.02
$\chi^2_1 = 0.20$	$\chi^2_4 = 2.06$	$\chi^2_1 = 0.06$	$\chi^2_4 = 0.89$
B-K-S = 0.23	b = 1 ~ $\chi^2_1 = 0.82$	B-K-S = 0.18	b = 1 ~ $\chi^2_1 = 2.08$

$$\text{Equation 7:} \left(\frac{M}{P}\right)_t = a + by_t + ci_t^* + \sum_{j=-k}^{k}[d_j\Delta y_{t-j} + e_j\Delta i^*_{t-j}] + \rho\left[\left(\frac{M}{P}\right)_{t-1} - a - by_{t-1} - ci^*_{t-1}\right] + \xi_t$$

Constant	−0.54	(−0.78)	Constant	0.16	(0.45)
y_t	0.36	(4.95)	y_t	0.41	(12.23)
i_t^*	−0.05	(−2.63)	i_t^*	−0.10	(−10.70)
Δy_{t-2}	−0.24	(−2.16)	Δy_t	0.08	(1.00)
Δi^*_{t-2}	−0.05	(−2.81)	Δi_t^*	0.05	(3.18)
Δy_{t-1}	−0.07	(−0.33)	Δy_{t+1}	−0.09	(−0.47)
Δi^*_{t-2}	−0.03	(−1.78)	Δi^*_{t+1}	−0.03	(−3.15)
Δy_t	−0.68	(−2.17)	ρ	−0.50	(−5.58)
Δi_t^*	0.01	(0.54)			
Δy_{t+1}	1.80	(3.10)			
Δi^*_{t+1}	0.03	(1.59)			
ρ	0.50	(−2.96)			

$\bar{R}^2 = 0.97$	SE = 0.03	$\bar{R}^2 = 0.99$	SE = 0.02
$\chi^2_1 = 0.31$	$\chi^2_4 = 2.89$	$\chi^2_1 = 0.40$	$\chi^2_4 = 0.89$
B-K-S = 0.16	b = 1 ~ $\chi^2_1 = 80.22$	B-K-S = 0.17	b = 1 ~ $\chi^2_1 = 308.05$

Sources: BCRD; and IMF staff estimates.

T ratios are in parentheses. Bartlett-Kolmogorov-Smirnov (B-K-S) 10 percent critical value is 0.305.

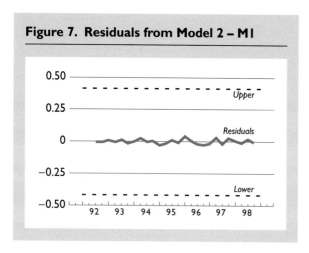

Figure 7. Residuals from Model 2 – M1

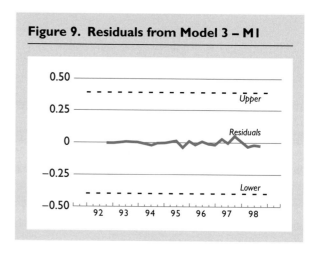

Figure 9. Residuals from Model 3 – M1

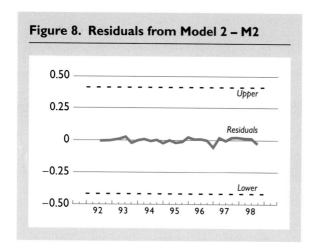

Figure 8. Residuals from Model 2 – M2

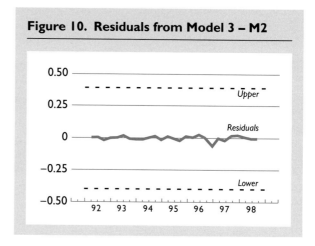

Figure 10. Residuals from Model 3 – M2

growth of real monetary aggregates equals the rate of productivity growth, that is, the rate of potential output growth. Given that the model assumes long-run money neutrality, the results of regressions (5) and (6) are not surprising. It could also be argued that a good representation of the *long-run* real demand for M1 seems consistent with a cash-in-advance model where money is a means of payment (Lucas and Stokey, 1987).

In contrast, the long-run interest rate semielasticity of real M2 is positive, and strongly significant, either with the domestic interest rate or with the interest rate differential. Its value, however, is small (0.05). The strongly significant *negative* interest semielasticity of the foreign interest rate (0.10) argues against the interpretation that the interest rate differential is driven mostly by the variance of the domestic interest rate. The significant positive interest semielasticity of real M2 may be due to the fact

that M2 includes the only domestic interest-bearing assets that economic agents have available in the Dominican Republic. It is also possible that this is the result of the frequent BCRD foreign exchange market interventions that, in the presence of large capital inflows, have tended to keep interest rates higher than otherwise.[80]

The coefficients on the interest rate *changes* reflect the short-run dynamics of the model. It is noteworthy that all significant coefficients of *changes* either in the domestic interest rate or in the interest rate differential (lagged, contemporaneous, led) are negative, as it is customary to find in money demand estimations

[80]The negative and significant real M1 and M2 long-run interest rate semielasticities with respect to the foreign interest rate may indicate that the domestic money function that matters for this version of money demand is the store-of-value function of money. Foreign currencies are not used as means of payment in the Dominican Republic.

(Johansen and Juselius, 1990). Moreover, they are not statistically different across specifications.

The negative coefficients of *changes* in the domestic interest rate (or in the interest rate differential), together with the positive long-run interest rate semielasticity of real M2 (and the zero long-run interest rate semielasticity of real M1), are consistent with the open economy paradigm of Mundell-Fleming. Those results suggest that the efficacy of monetary policy in the Dominican Republic, measured by its ability to affect domestic interest rates, is lower in the long run than in the short run.[81] A tightening of monetary policy, for instance, increases the domestic interest rate, encouraging capital inflows, and appreciates the currency.[82] If the authorities let the currency appreciate, as the banking system intermediates the capital inflow, real M2 increases and domestic credit also rises. If the monetary authorities intervene to prevent the appreciation of the exchange rate, the monetary base may increase (increasing real M2, other things being equal) as long as the intervention is unsterilized. If sterilized, the intervention would put upward pressure on interest rates, attracting further capital inflows.

The varying results for short- and long-run coefficients illustrate that in assessing the stance of monetary policy in open economies, it is important to distinguish the long-run equilibrium from the short-run dynamics.[83] Otherwise, the identification of the effects of policy shocks (and nonpolicy shocks) on interest rates is likely to be difficult. For example, a policy-induced monetary tightening will increase interest rates and reduce money demand in the short run. However, because of the feedback between interest rates and capital flows, we may find over time that the initial monetary tightening produces an increase in monetary aggregates. In addition, if inflation expectations embedded in interest rates decline (as they could with a monetary policy tightening), interest rates will eventually decline, although this should not be interpreted as a loosening of monetary policy.

Finally, the highly significant values of the coefficients measuring the previous-period deviation from long-run equilibrium indicate that adjustment to changes in the domestic interest rate or in the interest

rate differential takes place between two and four quarters. This is consistent with most accounts of the lags with which monetary policy normally operates in the Dominican Republic. The coefficient measuring the previous-period deviation from long-run equilibrium following a change in the foreign interest rate indicates that adjustment takes place relatively more rapidly; it takes place in one quarter.

Conclusion and Policy Implications

This study reports the estimation of three money demand equations for two real monetary aggregates (M1 and M2), one using the domestic interest rate, another using the interest rate differential between the 90-day domestic deposit rate and the 90-day U.S. treasury bill rate, and the last one using only the U.S. interest rate. The results suggest that in the sample period 1992:Q1–1999:Q1 there is cointegration between real monetary aggregates (M1 and M2), real output, and interest rates in any of the three forms used in this study.

The long-run income elasticity is not statistically different from one where the domestic interest rate, or the interest rate differential with the United States, is used. The long-run interest rate semielasticity, or the long-run interest rate differential semielasticity, is significant and positive for real M2 demand, but not for real M1 demand. The long-run semielasticities have a low value when the interest rate used is the domestic rate or the interest rate differential. In contrast, the long-run foreign interest rate semielasticity is negative and strongly significant for both real M1 and real M2. Real M2 is more responsive to the foreign interest rate than it is to the domestic interest rate.

By relating the overall results to the three motivations of this study, it can be concluded that, first, the data support the central role of money demand in the monetary program of the BCRD. Second, it seems that the efficacy of monetary policy in the Dominican Republic, measured by its ability in affecting the domestic interest rate in a lasting manner, is lower in the long run than in the short run. Finally, the monetary policy stance is not well measured by interest rates alone, or by the growth of monetary aggregates alone. As the varying results for short- and long-run coefficients illustrate, in assessing the stance of monetary policy in open economies, it is important to distinguish the long-run equilibrium from the short-run dynamics. Otherwise, the identification of the effects of policy shocks (and nonpolicy shocks) on interest rates is likely to be difficult, and lead to contradictory results, as the recent debate on the monetary policy stance in Asia shows.

---

[81]As stated earlier, the rapid growth of the economy during the sample period as well as the underdeveloped state of Dominican financial markets also suggest a positive interest rate semielasticity of real M2.

[82]Nadal-De Simone and Razzak (1994) found that increases in the interest rate differential between the United States and Germany, and between the United States and the United Kingdom, appreciated the U.S. dollar during the floating period.

[83]Goldfeld and Sichel (1990) have a fascinating account of problems referring to the interpretation of money demand estimates generated running regressions in levels and in first differences well before the use of cointegration analysis.

Despite the robustness of the results of the paper, it should be kept in mind that the short sample available prevented any meaningful stability test. Similarly, a meaningful out-of-sample simulation could not be performed. Finally, the use of the terms "long-run cointegration relationships" between real monetary aggregates, real output, and interest rates in this paper should be put in the context of the seven-year length of the sample available.[84]

_____

[84]However, seven years is already "the long run" for monetary policy.

Appendix VI.1   A Stylized Open Economy Model

This appendix uses a version of the standard textbook IS-LM model to illustrate the behavior of a small open economy following a monetary policy shock. In two recent articles, McCallum and Nelson (1996, 1999) showed that the standard IS-LM framework for a small open economy is compatible with explicit analysis of the maximizing behavior of rational economic agents, provided that the IS curve includes expected future output on the right-hand side, and that there is no habit formation in consumption.[85]

Assume a small open economy that produces two goods, some of which are exported. The economy also imports and consumes foreign goods. The price of domestic goods (p_t) is determined mostly by domestic forces while the price of foreign goods (p_t^*) is determined in world markets. With all variables except interest rates in logs, the model is

$$y_t^d = a_0 + E_t y_{t+1}^d + a_1 r_t + a_2 q_t + a_3 y_t^* + \varepsilon_t^{yd} \quad \text{(A1)}$$

$$r_t = i_t - E_t (P_{t+1} - P_t) \quad \text{(A2)}$$

$$q_t = e_t + p_t^* - p_t \quad \text{(A3)}$$

$$y_t^s = \bar{y}_t + d_1 (p_t - E_{t-1} \bar{p}_t) + \varepsilon_t^{ys} \quad \text{(A4)}$$

$$\bar{y}_t = \delta + \varepsilon_t^{\bar{y}} \quad \text{(A5)}$$

$$P_t = \alpha p_t + (1 - \alpha)(e_t + p_t^*) \quad \text{(A6)}$$

$$m_t - P_t = b_0 + b_1 y_t + b_2 i_t + \varepsilon_t^{md} \quad \text{(A7)}$$

$$i_t = i_t^* + E_t (e_{t+1} - e_t) + \rho \quad \text{(A8)}$$

$$m_t = c_0 + \Gamma m_{t-1} + \varepsilon_t^{ms} \quad \text{(A9)}$$

where y_t^d is the demand for the domestic good, a_0 is a constant, r_t is the real interest rate, q_t is the real exchange rate, y_t^* is foreign output, e_t is the nominal exchange rate (defined as the number of domestic currency units necessary to buy a unit of foreign currency), p_t^* is the price of foreign output, p_t is the price of domestic goods, $\bar{y}_t$ is potential output, δ is a constant productivity rate, P_t is the general price level as measured by the consumer price index, α is the share of domestic goods in the price index, m_t is the money stock, b_0 is a constant, i_t is the nominal interest rate, i_t^* is the foreign nominal interest rate, ρ is a constant country risk premium, and c_0 is a constant. E_i is the expectational operator based on information available at time i. All disturbance terms, ε_t, are assumed to be white noise for simplicity. All coefficients except a_1 and b_2 are positive.

Equation (A1) is an IS curve for a small open economy that includes the expected value of next period's output as suggested by McCallum and Nelson. Equation (A2) is the Fisher equation; there is an identical relation for the rest of the world. Equation (A3) defines the real exchange rate. Equations (A2) and (A3) represent real interest rate parity.[86]

Aggregate supply behavior is represented by equation (A4), which embodies the "natural rate" hypothesis. Following McCallum and Nelson (1996), "price stickiness" is introduced simply by assuming that producers set domestic goods prices in period t at the value ($\bar{p}_t$) that is expected to clear the market $p_t = E_{t-1} \bar{p}_t$, given information available at time (t–1). The idea is that market participants find it optimal to pre-set prices at levels that are expected to clear the market next period.[87] Therefore, p_t is the price that would prevail in the goods market if there were no unexpected shocks. Unexpected demand and supply shocks will make output realizations different from expected values. As a result, current period output is demand-determined given the price preset for the current period by producers, based on their information at the end of previous period.

While the standard IS-LM model is frequently regarded as implying the existence of capital adjustment costs, the model here has no explicit capital adjustment costs. Therefore, equation (A5) assumes that potential output ($\bar{y}_t$), consistent with the assumption that there are no contemporaneous responses of output to monetary shocks, grows at the exogenously given productivity rate δ.[88]

---

[85]See the discussion of McCallum and Nelson's model in Walsh (1998).

[86]It is assumed that the rates of return on domestic and foreign assets are measured in the same units.

[87]This assumption could presumably be justified by the existence of menu costs or, more generally, by the costs of gathering and processing information (Brunner and others, 1983).

[88]See McCallum and Nelson (2000) for a similar argument.

Equation (A6) defines the overall price level in terms of the prices of domestic and foreign goods. Equation (A7) describes the demand for money. Equation (A8) is uncovered interest parity, and assumes a constant country risk premium for simplicity.[89] Equation (A9) describes the behavior of the nominal money supply which follows an AR(1) process such that when $\Gamma = 1$, the monetary shock is permanent, and when $\Gamma \neq 1$, the monetary shock is transitory.

After some algebra and assuming for simplicity zero expected inflation abroad,

$$y_t^d = a_0 + E_t^y d_{t+1} + a_1[i_t - E_t(P_{t+1} - P_t)] + \quad \text{(A10)}$$
$$a_2(e_t + p_t^* - p_t) + a_3 y_t^* + \varepsilon_t^{y^d}$$

$$y_t^s = \delta + d_1(p_t - E_{t-1}\bar{p}_t) + \varepsilon_t^{y^s} \quad \text{(A11)}$$

$$m_t - P_t = b_0 + b_1 y_t + b_2[i_t^* + \quad \text{(A12)}$$
$$E_t(e_{t+1} - e_t)] + \varepsilon_t^{m^d}$$

Equations (A10)–(A12) determine the price and the output of the domestic good, together with the exchange rate (or the interest rate via interest rate parity).[90] Various versions of equation (A12) were estimated.[91]

To illustrate the behavior of the economy, it is convenient to view the expected value of a variable as its long-run value. For example, $E_t e_{t+1}$ is the long run value of the nominal exchange rate, the value that will prevail under full employment and full price adjustment.

The behavior of the economy described by the system (A10)–(A12) is exhibited in Figures 11 and 12. In the upper panels, all output-interest rate combinations for which there is equilibrium in the goods market and in the money market are represented by the downward-sloping IS curve and the upward-sloping LM curve, respectively. The upward-sloping BP curve in the upper panels describes all the output-interest rate combinations for which there is balance of payments equilibrium. The BP curve is less steep than the LM curve to indicate a large degree of capital mobility (normally, a BP curve steeper than an LM curve is used to represent a case of low capital mobility). The larger the increase is in the capital inflow for a given increase in the interest rate, the smaller will be the increase in the interest rate required to maintain balance of payments equilibrium as output rises; that is, the flatter the BP curve will

[89]Frankel's (1991) terminology is used here. In a set of developed and developing countries, Frankel finds that most of the variance in the real interest rate differential is explained by expected changes in the real exchange rate (currency risk) rather than by the slowly changing covered interest rate parity (country risk).

[90]A similar model is solved and simulated in Nadal-De Simone (2001).

[91]The constant term includes the constant risk premium.

Figure 11. A Transitory Monetary Expansion

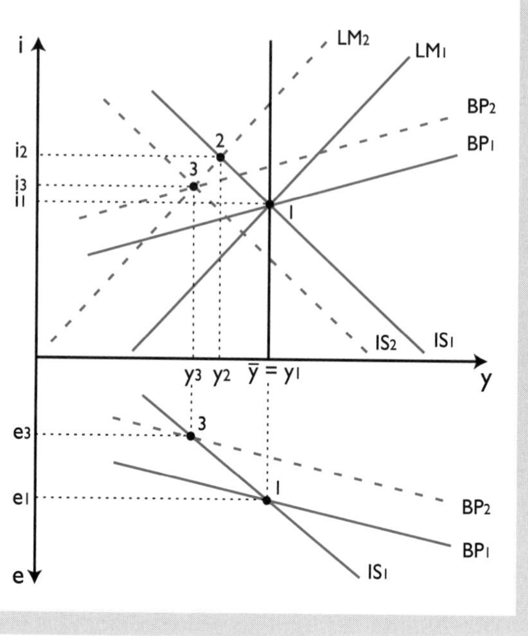

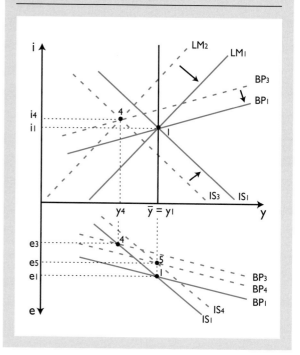

Figure 12. A Permanent Monetary Expansion

be. In the lower panels, upward-sloping IS and BP curves show all the combinations of exchange rates and output for which there is equilibrium in the goods market and in the balance of payments.

Figure 11 shows the behavior of the economy following a temporary reduction in the money supply, that is, all expected values equal their long-run equilibrium levels. A monetary tightening—prior to the change in the exchange rate—increases the interest rate from i_1 to i_2, decreases output to y_2, and the balance of payments shows an incipient surplus. Point 2 is not an equilibrium. As a result, the exchange rate appreciates from e_1 to e_3 to preserve interest rate parity. The interest rate falls somewhat to i_3 as capital flows in. The appreciation of the exchange rate shifts the BP curve upward and restores balance of payments equilibrium. The appreciation of the exchange rate also shifts the IS curve downward because imports rise and exports fall. Output falls further to y_3. After the temporary monetary contraction, the economy has moved from point 1 to point 3, where output is below potential. As the contractionary monetary policy is reversed over time, the economy will return to point 1.

In Figure 12, because the monetary tightening is permanent, not only the exchange rate but also the expected exchange rate will appreciate. As a result, the increase in the interest rate, the fall in output, and the spot exchange rate appreciation are larger than in the case of the temporary monetary shock. Point 4 is the new short-run equilibrium. However, at point 4, output is below potential. Thus, over time, domestic prices will start to fall to their new long-run equilibrium. That reduction will be proportional to the fall in the money supply. The fall in prices discourages imports and encourages exports, and therefore the IS and BP curves move to the right. Because the fall in prices increases real money balances, LM shifts downward, and the interest rate falls. The curves stop shifting when the price level and the exchange rate fall in proportion to the fall in the money supply and output is back to potential. The new equilibrium will be at point 1 in the upper panel, and at 5 in the lower panel.

If the monetary authority partially offsets the exchange rate appreciation that follows the monetary policy tightening via an unsterilized intervention in the foreign exchange market, the stock of money will be relatively larger and the interest rate will be relatively lower than otherwise. As a result, the money stock behavior will be endogenized and, in the short run, all the curves will shift relatively less than in the case of a pure exchange rate float.

Appendix VI.2   Unit Roots and Cointegration

The literature on unit roots and cointegration is vast and will not be reviewed here. Suffice it to say that there is a valid concern among economists about the appropriateness of the tests for unit roots and their power against stationary alternatives. The choice of a particular testing methodology is not straightforward. Ultimately, one may not be able to determine whether there is a unit root in a given time series. Inevitably, however, a choice has to be made. In testing for unit roots and cointegration, the strategy followed in this study was to use different tests. A decision was then made based on whether or not the results of these various tests converge. Two popular methods to test unit roots were used: the ADF test (Dickey and Fuller, 1979, 1981, and Said and Dickey, 1984), and the Phillips-Perron test (Phillips, 1987, and Perron, 1988). Given the behavior of the 90-day T-bill rate in the period 1994–1995, the Perron (1997) test, which allows for a break in the intercept and or the slope of the series, was used for that series.

Tables 30 and 31 report the results for unit root tests.[92] In general, the tests considered tend to agree that real M1, real M2, the domestic interest rate, the interest rate differential, and the foreign interest rate are unit root processes. However, while the T_μ and the T_τ versions of the ADF and the Phillips-Perron tests reject the null of a unit root in real output, the ρ_μ and the ρ_τ versions of those tests accept the null. As the latter versions of the tests are more powerful against a stationary alternative, it was decided that real output may contain a unit root. That decision was also based on the observation that the spectrum of the first difference of real output has Granger's typical spectral shape.[93]

Gonzalo (1994) compared five different residual-based tests for cointegration. Among them, he recommends using the Johansen-Juselius (1990) method. Although very popular in the literature, this test has been highly criticized for its lack of power in finite samples, and—among other problems—by its sensitivity to the choice of the lag length. This test was used and the results are reported in Table 32. Given the relatively short sample period available, the critical values were corrected for small sample bias using Cheung and Lai's (1993) approach. Lag length was evaluated as follows. A general lag model was estimated. Then, unnecessary lags were eliminated by testing backward using the Schwarz Criterion. The residuals of the models were checked for white noise each time using LM(1) and LM(4) tests, and for normality using a multivariate version of the Shenton-Bowman test. In all cases the tests accepted the null of Gaussian residuals. The LM(1) tests for real M2-domestic interest rate, real M2-interest rate differential, and real M1-foreign interest rate indicated some serial correlation. The LM(4) tests—and LM tests with longer lags—however, accepted the null of white noise for the residuals at reasonable confidence levels.

At the 99 percent level and in all cases analyzed in this study, the λ_{trace} statistic strongly rejected the null hypothesis of no cointegrating vectors against the alternative of one or more cointegrating vectors ($r > 0$). Similarly, at the 99 percent level and in all cases, the λ_{max} statistic rejected the null hypothesis of no cointegrating vectors against the alternative of one cointegrating vector ($r = 1$). For M2, the λ_{trace} statistic rejected the null hypothesis of $r \leq 1$ cointegrating vectors against the alternative of two or more cointegrating vectors at the 95 percent level, except when the foreign interest rate was used. For M1, that rejection occurred at the 90 percent level, again with exception of the system with the foreign interest rate. The λ_{max} statistics rejected the null of one cointegrating vector ($r = 1$) against the specific alternative of two cointegrating vectors ($r = 2$) at the 95 percent level at least in all cases, except in the case of real M1 and the foreign interest rate.[94]

Finally, if real output were stationary, one more cointegrating vector would be required. As a result,

---

[92]The choice of the lag structure always has been an issue. The objective of the lags is to remove serial correlation. With this objective in mind, the lag order was set as the highest significant lag order—using an approximate 95 percent confidence interval—from either the autocorrelation function or the partial autocorrelation function of the first-differenced series. Also the Akaike Information Criterion was used. Every time a lag was eliminated, serial correlation was checked using the Ljung-Box test for white noise. The approach followed in selecting the lags was also followed in testing nonstationarity in the individual series.

[93]Results are available upon request.

[94]The λ_{max} statistic has a sharper alternative hypothesis than the λ_{trace} statistic. In case of conflict, the former is to be preferred to the latter.

multivariate tests of nonstationarity were performed. They did not reject the null of a unit root for real output when the aggregate was real M1, but they did reject the null of a unit root for real output in the case of real M2. This confirmed the decision taken based on Dickey-Fuller and Phillips-Perron tests for the case of M1. As a result, real GDP was also detrended assuming a deterministic trend, and all the cointegration tests were run again. At the 99 percent level, the λ_{max} statistic rejected the null hypothesis of two cointegrating vectors against the alternative of three cointegrating vectors for real M2 and the domestic interest rate. That rejection occurred at the 95 percent level for real M2 and the interest rate differential.

References

Blinder, A.S., 1998, *Central Banking in Theory and Practice,* Cambridge, Massachusetts: The MIT Press.

Brunner, K., A., Cukierman, and A. Meltzer, 1983, "Money and Economic Activity: Inventories and Business Cycles," *Journal of Monetary Economics,* Vol. 11, pp. 281–319.

Cheung, Y.W., and K.S. Lai, 1993, "Finite Sample Sizes of Johansen's Likelihood Ratio Test for Cointegration," *Oxford Bulletin of Economics and Statistics,* Vol. 55, pp. 313–28.

Christiano, L.J., M. Eichenbaum, and C.L. Evans, 1998, "Monetary Policy Shocks: What Have We Learned and to What End?," *National Bureau of Economic Research,* Working Paper No. 6400.

Corsetti, G., P. Pesenti, and N. Roubini, 1998, "What Caused the Asian Currency and Financial Crisis? Part II: The Policy Debate," *National Bureau of Economic Research,* Working Paper No. 6834.

Cuddington, J.T., 1983, "Currency Substitution, Capital Mobility, and Money Demand," *Journal of International Money and Finance,* Vol. 2, pp. 111–33.

Dickey, D., and W.A. Fuller, 1979, "Distribution of Estimates for Autoregressive Time Series with Unit Root," *Journal of American Statistical Association,* Vol. 74, pp. 427–31.

———, 1981, "The Likelihood Ratio Statistic for Autoregressive Time Series with a Unit Root," *Econometrica,* Vol. 49, pp. 1057–72.

Frankel, J., 1991, "Quantifying Capital Mobility in the 1980s," in B.D. Berheim and J.B. Shoven (eds.) *National Saving and Economic Performance* (The University of Chicago Press).

Goldfeld, S.M., and D.E. Sichel, 1990, "The Demand for Money," in B.M. Friedman and F.H. Hahn (eds.) *Handbook of Monetary Economics* (Amsterdam: North Holland).

Gonzalo, J., 1994, "Five Alternative Methods of Estimating Long-Run Equilibrium Relationships," *Journal of Econometrics,* Vol. 60, pp. 203–33.

Johansen, S., and K. Juselius, 1990, "Maximum Likelihood Estimation and Inference on Cointegration—With Application to the Demand for Money," *Oxford Bulletin of Economics and Statistics,* Vol. 52, pp. 169–210.

Laidler, D.E.W., 1994, *The Demand for Money: Theories, Evidence and Problems,* fourth ed., (New York: Harper-Collins).

Leiderman, L., and L.O. Svensson (eds.), 1995, *Inflation Targets* (London: Centre for Economic Policy Research).

Lucas, R.E., and N. Stokey, 1987, "Money and Interest in a Cash-in Advance Economy," *Econometrica,* Vol. 55, pp. 491–514.

McCallum, B.T., 1996, *International Monetary Economics* (Oxford University Press).

———, and E. Nelson, 2000, "An Optimizing IS-LM Specification for Monetary Policy and Business Cycle Analysis," National Bureau of Economic Research, Working Paper No. 5875.

———, 1999, "Nominal Income Targeting in an Open Economy Optimizing Model," *Journal of Monetary Economics,* Vol. 43, pp. 553–78.

Mundell, R.A., 1963, "Capital Mobility and Stabilization Policy Under Fixed and Flexible Exchange Rates," *Canadian Journal of Economics and Political Science,* 29, pp. 475–85.

Nadal-De Simone, F., 2001, "Inflation Targeting in a Small Open Economy: The Behaviour of Price Variables," *New Zealand Economic Papers,* Vol. 35, pp. 101–42.

———, and W. Razzak, 1999, "Nominal Exchange Rates and Nominal Interest Rate Differentials," Working Paper WP/99/141 (Washington: International Monetary Fund).

Perron, P., 1988, "Trends and Random Walks in Macroeconomic Time Series," *Journal of Economic Dynamics and Control,* Vol. 12, pp. 297–32.

———, 1997, "Further Evidence on Breaking Trend Functions in Macroeconomic Variables," *Journal of Econometrics,* Vol. 80, pp. 355–85.

Phillips, P.C.B., 1987, "Time Series Regressions with a Unit Root," *Econometrica,* Vol. 55, pp. 277–301.

———, and M. Loretan, 1991, "Estimating Long-Run Equilibria," *The Review of Economic Studies,* Vol. 58, pp. 407–36.

Said, S., and D.A. Dickey, 1984, "Testing for Unit Roots in Autoregressive-Moving Average Models of Unknown Order," *Biometrika,* Vol. 71, pp. 599–608.

Siklos, P., 1996, "Searching for an Improved Monetary Indicator for New Zealand," Discussion Papers Series G96/1, (Wellington: Reserve Bank of New Zealand).

Tanner, E., 1999, "Exchange Market Pressure and Monetary Policy: Asia and Latin America in the 1990s," unpublished, (Washington: International Monetary Fund).

Walsh, C., 1998, *Monetary Theory and Policy* (MIT Press).

VII Exchange Market Pressure, Monetary Policy, and Interest Rates: Recent Evidence from the Dominican Republic

Recently, the authorities of the Dominican Republic have permitted more exchange rate flexibility while attempting to increase gross official reserves. Under a managed float, as in the Dominican Republic, it is inappropriate when assessing the stance of monetary policy to examine either of these variables (exchange rate and reserve changes) in isolation. Instead, exchange rate and reserve movements should be combined to form a measure of exchange market pressure (EMP), which is defined as the sum of exchange rate depreciation and outflows of official international reserves.

Under a managed float, contractionary monetary policy should, all else being equal, attract capital inflows (raising official reserves) and increase the value of the Dominican peso, thereby reducing EMP. However, over time, lower EMP should increase investor confidence and ultimately reduce the differential between domestic and foreign interest rates.

This chapter examines several questions related to monetary policy and EMP in the Dominican Republic. First, according to the historical record, does monetary policy affect EMP in the way that standard monetary frameworks would predict? For example, has contractionary monetary policy been successful in either defending the peso or increasing international reserves? Second, and closely related, how should the stance of monetary policy be measured? While most recent work uses an interest rate as the policy variable, this chapter emphasizes changes in the domestic credit component of the monetary base, as in the traditional monetary approach to the balance of payments. Third, is the interest rate differential itself a function of EMP? Does lower EMP boost investor confidence and thus reduce the interest rate differential? Fourth, is the stance of monetary policy itself a function of EMP? Do the monetary authorities respond to changes in EMP with monetary expansions or contractions? Do the monetary authorities systematically sterilize changes of EMP with changes in domestic credit, as in several other emerging markets?[95]

To address such questions, this chapter develops a VAR framework with three variables, namely EMP, domestic credit growth, and the interest rate differential.[96] This methodology is well suited to address the above questions since it pinpoints "shocks" or "innovations" to the variables mentioned above, estimates the responses to shocks between these variables, both contemporaneously and on a lagged basis, and summarizes how monetary policy (as measured by domestic credit growth) responds to lagged changes in either EMP or the interest differential.

Several policy-relevant conclusions (with numerical estimates) will be presented. First, the growth of central bank credit (scaled by base money) is a good indicator of the stance of monetary policy in the Dominican Republic. Second, monetary policy affects EMP significantly and in the direction predicted by theory. For example, a tightening of monetary policy, that is a reduction in central bank credit growth, reduces EMP, both immediately and, to a lesser degree, within a one- to five-month period. Third, domestic monetary policy had an ambiguous effect on the interest differential. Contractionary (expansionary) monetary policy is generally associated with interest rate increases (decreases). However, an effect in the opposite direction can also occur, since monetary expansions (contractions) can raise (lower) inflation expectations and cause interest rates to rise (fall). Moreover, reductions in EMP were associated with a lagged reduction in the interest rate differential, possibly reflecting increased investor confidence.

Exchange Market Pressure in the Dominican Republic: An Overview

Prior to 1991, the Dominican Republic fixed the official exchange rate,[97] but devalued periodically. In

---

[95]Such behavior has been discussed recently in the context of balance of payments crises (Flood, Garber, and Kramer, 1996). For empirical evidence related to this issue in Mexico during the

1994–95 crisis, see Calvo and Mendoza (1996). For evidence on this issue in other countries, see Tanner (2001).

[96]In a monetary framework, a scale variable for money demand should also be included. Most frequently, this variable is GDP. However, this study uses monthly data, for which neither GDP nor industrial production data are available.

[97]Defined in Dominican pesos per U.S. dollar throughout this chapter.

late 1991, the authorities abandoned the fixed peg in favor of smaller, more frequent exchange rate movements. While the exchange rate has never floated freely, it has become more flexible in recent years. Between January 1992 and August 1994 monthly exchange rate depreciation averaged 0.15 percent. Subsequently, average monthly exchange rate depreciation was 0.35 percent, mainly reflecting devaluations in 1997 and 1998.

Under such a managed exchange rate regime, EMP is reflected in both exchange rate and reserve movements. Girton and Roper (1977) showed that EMP is the flow excess supply of money. To see this, consider the following simple monetary model. On the demand side, the growth of real base money (m_t) is:

$$m_t = \Delta M_t / M_{t-1} - \pi_t \qquad (1)$$

where M_t is nominal (base) money at time t and π_t is the inflation rate ($\Delta P_t / P_{t-1}$, where P_t is the price level at time t). The inflation rate is linked to foreign inflation π_t^* through the rate of growth of the nominal exchange rate e_t:

$$e_t = \pi_t - \pi_t^* + z_t \qquad (2)$$

where z_t is the deviation from purchasing power parity.

On the supply side, the two components of nominal base money are international reserves R_t and net domestic assets D_t. Thus,

$$\Delta M_t / M_{t-1} = (\Delta R_t + \Delta D_t) / M_{t-1} = r_t + \delta_t \qquad (3)$$

where $r_t = \Delta R_t / M_{t-1}$ and $\delta_t = \Delta D_t / M_{t-1}$. The above equations restate the traditional monetary approach. Assuming that purchasing power parity holds and foreign inflation equals zero ($z_t = \pi_t^* = 0$), substitute (2) and (3) into (1) and rearrange to obtain an expression for EMP:

$$e_t - r_t = \delta_t - m_t \qquad (4)$$

According to equation (4), exchange rate depreciation plus reserve outflows (scaled by base money) equals the difference between the growth rates of the domestic component of the monetary base (δ_t) and money demand (m_t).[98] Under a fixed exchange rate regime, $e_t = 0$; with freely floating exchange rates, $r_t = 0$.[99]

Table 34 and Figure 13 present data on EMP, exchange rate growth, gross international reserves, and the interest rate differential in the Dominican Republic for the period 1992–98 and selected subperiods.[100] These data show that EMP in the Dominican Republic primarily represents reserve movements rather than exchange rate depreciation. The data also suggest that EMP is higher in the early years of the decade than subsequently. Severe pressures, associated with an electoral campaign, occur between August 1993 and August 1994. During this period gross reserves fell by about US$440 million (from about US$640 million to just under US$200 million), and

[98]This definition may also be obtained for the more general case of non-zero π^*. An even more general definition of EMP ($e - \alpha r$) where α is reduced-form coefficient that depends on several underlying structural parameters. Under standard assumptions of the monetary approach to exchange rates and the balance of payments, α should be unity. Subsequently, other authors relaxed these assumptions (see, for example, Weymark, 1998) and found that α might be difficult to obtain. Therefore, α is nonetheless commonly set to unity, as doing so yields an informative indicator (although perhaps not one consistent with a deeper structural model).

[99]This framework also applies to freely floating exchange rates that are subject to a reserve growth target.

[100]All data are from the IMF's *International Financial Statistics,* international reserves are defined by series 11.d, gross reserves excluding gold. The monetary base is series 14. Domestic credit is defined as the difference between the monetary base and net foreign assets (series 14 minus series 11 plus series 16c).

Table 34. Exchange Market Pressure and Related Variables

(Period averages, in percent)

Year/Month	EMP	Reserves Loss $\Delta R/M$	Exchange Rate Depreciation $\Delta E/E$	Interest Rate Differential (ϕ)	Credit Growth (δ)
1992–1998	0.37	0.10	0.27	8.84	0.92
1992:1–1993:7	−0.95	−0.96	0.01	12.47	0.14
1993:8–1994:8	3.39	3.03	0.35	6.68	3.39
1994:9–1998:10	0.08	−0.27	0.36	8.01	0.56

Sources: BCRD; and IMF staff estimates.

Notes: 1. EMP is defined as exchange rate depreciation plus change in international reserves divided by monetary base. 2. Interest rate differential (ϕ) is domestic currency deposit rate minus U.S. (Libor) rate (3-month). 3. Credit variable (δ) is change in central bank credit divided by the monetary base. EMP and δ are percent per month; interest rates are percent per year.

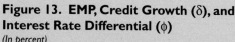

Figure 13. EMP, Credit Growth (δ), and Interest Rate Differential (ϕ)
(In percent)

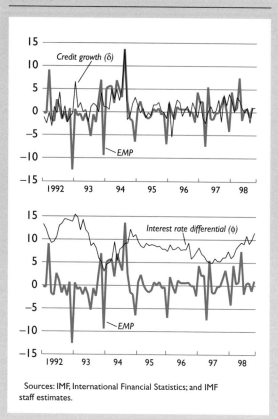

Sources: IMF, International Financial Statistics; and IMF staff estimates.

Note that the coefficient on δ_t statistically differs from zero at the 99 percent level. Presumably, there should also be a relationship between lagged δ and EMP_t. However, the regression above examines only the contemporaneous relationship between δ_t and EMP_t. (The relationship between δ and EMP over time is explored in the next section.) According to the adjusted R^2 statistic, on a contemporaneous basis alone, 17 percent of EMP is explained by movements in δ_t.

This finding suggests that δ is an appropriate measure of the stance of monetary policy. However, in much recent work on monetary policy, many authors have used an interest rate, rather than a monetary aggregate like δ, to gauge the stance of monetary policy.[102] For a small relatively open economy like the Dominican Republic, the differential between domestic and foreign (U.S.) interest rates ϕ_t conveys important information: it indicates both expected exchange rate depreciation and a premium required to satisfy the marginal investor. Thus, all else being constant, an increase in ϕ_t (due to contractionary monetary policy) encourages capital inflows and reduces EMP. In theory, the relationship between ϕ and EMP is ambiguous. On the one hand, an increase in ϕ_t may signal anticipated exchange rate depreciation (a Fisher effect) and/or higher risk, reflecting loose monetary policy. In the Dominican Republic, casual inspection suggests that, unlike δ_t, ϕ_t does not appear to be closely correlated with EMP_t, either visually (see Figure 13) or in bivariate regressions.[103]

EMP averaged over 3 percent per month, peaking at 13 percent in August 1994 (compared with an average of less than 1 percent for the 1990–98 period as whole). Thereafter, EMP falls and becomes less variable, despite devaluations in 1997 and 1998.

A key determinant of EMP is δ_t, the growth of the domestic component of the monetary base. If monetary policy is expansionary ($\delta_t > m_t$), EMP will rise (through some combination of reserve movements and exchange rate depreciation). In the Dominican Republic EMP_t and δ_t appear to move together. A positive correlation between EMP_t and δ_t is indicated both by visual inspection (see Figure 13, top) and a simple univariate regression (t-statistics in parenthesis):[101]

$$EMP_t = -0.24 + 0.648\,\delta_t \qquad (5)$$
$$(-0.57) \qquad (4.17)$$
$$R^2(\text{adjusted}) = 0.17$$
$$\text{Durbin-Watson Statistic} = 2.09$$

EMP and Monetary Policy: A Vector Autoregression Approach

As discussed above, one question that this chapter seeks to answer is whether monetary policy in the Dominican Republic affects EMP in the direction predicted by standard monetary theory. In this section, a vector autoregression framework is developed to address this question.

Consider the following VAR system:

$$X_t = a_0 + a_1 X_{t-1} + a_2 X_{t-2} + \ldots + v_t \qquad (6)$$

---

[101]Both EMP and δ are stationary. Hence, the regression does not represent a long-run (cointegrating) relationship.

[102]For example, for the United States, many authors, including Bernanke and Blinder (1992), argue that the stance of the Federal Reserve is best measured by the federal funds rate: higher interest rates reflect tighter monetary policy. In the context of developing countries, most authors have also used an interest rate to capture the stance of monetary policy. For example, in the case of Asia, several authors, including Radelet and Sachs (1998), Furman and Stiglitz (1998), Goldfajn and Baig (1998), and Goldfajn and Gupta (1998) do so.

[103]Results not reported here indicate, however, that ϕ and the level of international reserves are negatively cointegrated, suggesting that higher reserve holdings reduce risk and the risk premium.

where $X = (\delta, EMP, \phi)$ is a matrix of variables, a_i is a vector of coefficients, and $v_t = (v_\delta, v_E, v_\phi)$ is a vector of error terms.[104] A system like (6) permits testing for effects of past values of X on current values. Assumptions regarding the exogeneity of certain variables (like a policy variable) are easily incorporated into a system like (6). To do so, first assume that each element of the error vector v_t is in turn composed of "own" error terms $w_t = (w_\delta, w_E, w_\phi)$ and contemporaneous correlations with "other" errors. That is:

$$v_t = Bw_t \qquad (7)$$

where B is a 3×3 matrix whose diagonal elements ("own correlations") equal one and whose nonzero off-diagonal elements reflect contemporaneous correlations among the error terms. Now assumptions regarding the exogeneity of certain variables may be incorporated in restrictions on the matrix B.[105]

As discussed above, the domestic credit growth variable δ is assumed to be exogenous. That is, *in any period,* the residual δ (that is, v_δ) reflect only the tastes and preferences of the policymaker:

$$v_{\delta t} = w_{\delta t} \qquad (8)$$

Next, errors to exchange market pressure (v_E) contain two elements: the "own" shock (w_E) plus one related to innovations in domestic credit:

$$v_{Et} = w_{Et} + b_{21}w_{\delta t} \qquad (9)$$

Thus, w_E may be thought of as a shock to the demand for a country's currency, due perhaps to changes in investor confidence and sentiment. Thus $b_{21}w_{\delta t}$ represents the portion of shocks to EMP that is contemporaneously correlated with domestic credit growth.

Finally, errors to the change in the interest rate differential (w_ϕ) include the sum of three elements: the "own" shock (w_E) plus ones related to innovations in domestic credit and EMP:

$$v_{\phi t} = w_{\phi t} + b_{31}w_{\delta t} + b_{32}w_{Et} \qquad (10)$$

According to equation (10), innovations to domestic credit w_δ affect the interest rate differential through either standard liquidity or Fisher channels. (Thus, the predicted sign of b_{31} is ambiguous.) Second, the interest rate differential should respond to changes in EMP: a rise in EMP may signal either further exchange rate depreciation in the future, or additional risk, or both. Such effects are captured in the term $b_{32}w_{Et}$ and b_{32} should be greater than zero. The "own" shock w_ϕ thus contains other factors not

contained in either w_δ or w_E. This component should be thought of as a "hybrid" that potentially contains both policy- and market-determined elements.[106]

In addition to the contemporaneous relationships shown in equations (8)–(10), impulse response functions (IRFs) summarize the effect of past innovations (that is, *lagged* elements of w) to current values of X. Thus, IRFs provide two additional ways to evaluate the effect of monetary policy on EMP. First, IRFs show effects on EMP of both current and past innovations to domestic credit (w_δ). Second, IRFs also show effects on EMP of past (but not current) innovations to the interest rate differential (w_ϕ). But this latter IRF may only be thought of as a policy relationship insofar as innovations to the interest rate differential represent policy shocks. (Note also that IRFs show effects on $\Delta\phi$ of both current and past innovations to domestic credit and EMP, $[w_\delta]$ and $[w_E]$, respectively.)

The framework discussed above, however, also helps address the chapter's third main question, namely, how the stance of monetary policy is determined. Specifically, the IRFs provide a *policy reaction function:* they show effects on current δ of past (but not current) innovations to EMP (w_E) and changes in the interest rate differential ($w_{\phi t}$).[107] For example, when faced by positive innovations to EMP (such as a decrease in investor confidence) policymakers may respond "prudently" with contractionary policy (reducing δ). Policymakers might, however, face pressures to act otherwise. For example, when EMP rises, the authorities might also face pressures to provide liquidity to the domestic financial system (raising δ). Such a response, in the context of balance of payments crises and speculative attacks, is discussed in several papers, including Flood, Garber, and Kramer (1996) and Calvo and Mendoza (1996).

Estimation Results

Estimation results are presented in Table 35, Part A. These include adjusted R-squared statistics, exclusion (Granger causality) tests, and IRFs. IRFs are also presented graphically in Table 35, Part B, and Figures 14 through 16.

---

[104]Since ϕ_t is nonstationary in levels but stationary in first differences, it is entered accordingly as $\Delta\phi$.

[105]To implement these restrictions, either a Choleski decomposition or a procedure like Bernanke's (1986) may be used. For a review of issues regarding the estimation and identification of vector autoregressions, see also Enders (1995), Chapter V.

[106]An alternative assumption would be for EMP to be contemporaneously determined by both δ and $\Delta\phi$. In this case equation (9) would be rewritten as: $v_{Et} = w_{Et} + b_{21}w_{\delta t} + b_{23}w_{\phi t}$. Since ϕ reflects the opportunity cost of holding money, $b_{23} > 0$. Under this assumption, however, for the system also to be just identified, b_{31} must be zero in equation (10).

[107]Note that the issue addressed here is similar to that of exchange rate targeting. For example, Edwards and Savastano (1998) also estimate a policy reaction function for Mexico during the mid-1990s. However, they examine the effect of changes in the exchange rate (rather than EMP) on M1 (rather than domestic credit of the central bank).

Table 35. Summary of Estimates, Vector Autoregression System Equation (6)
1992–98 (Monthly Data)

$$(6) \qquad X_t = a_0 + a_1 X_{t-1} + a_2 X_{t-2} + \dots + v_t, \qquad X = (\delta, EMP, \Delta\phi)$$

A. F-tests for exclusion (P-statistics in parentheses)

Dependent Variable	δ	EMP	$\Delta\phi$
F-Test, exclusion of:			
Lagged δ	0.36 (0.84)	1.90 (0.12)	0.17 (0.96)
Lagged EMP	0.39 (0.81)	0.60 (0.67)	1.57 (0.19)
Lagged $\Delta\phi$	0.76 (0.55)	2.67 (0.04)	2.21 (0.08)
R^2 adjusted	−0.05	0.12	0.05

B. Impulse response functions (T-statistics in parentheses)

	Responses of					
	EMP		$\Delta\phi$		δ	
Shock to	δ	$\Delta\phi$	δ	EMP	EMP	$\Delta\phi$
Period 0	1.43 (4.23)	— —	0.09 (0.52)	0.16 (1.12)	— —	— —
Period 1	0.73 (1.80)	0.38 (0.89)	0.07 (0.43)	−0.03 (−0.19)	−0.07 (−0.26)	0.27 (0.94)
Period 2	0.75 (1.71)	0.36 (0.94)	0.05 (0.30)	0.34 (2.19)	0.33 (1.13)	0.06 (0.21)
Period 3	0.63 (1.54)	−1.05 (−2.32)	0.13 (0.86)	0.05 (0.36)	0.08 (0.33)	−0.34 (−1.21)
Period 4	−0.16 (−0.36)	0.40 (0.98)	0.04 (0.24)	−0.03 (−0.17)	0.15 (0.62)	0.26 (0.98)
Period 5	0.37 (1.08)	−0.27 (−0.88)	0.11 (1.00)	0.07 (0.69)	−0.06 (−0.40)	−0.15 (−0.89)

Sources: BCRD; and IMF staff estimates.

Note: For all estimates, 4 lags are used. P-statistics in parentheses. δ = growth of domestic credit (scaled by base money). EMP = exchange rate depreciation plus reserves loss (scaled by base money), $\Delta\phi$ = change in interest rate differential.

Importantly, estimates confirm that shocks to domestic credit growth (w_δ) affect EMP positively, as expected. As Table 35, Part A shows, the hypothesis that lagged δ does not help explain current EMP is not rejected at conventional levels. Nonetheless (see Table 35, Part B, and Figure 14, top) the current period (period 0) IRF is positive and significantly different from zero at the 99 percent level.[108] The results suggest that, contemporaneously, a 1 percent increase (decrease) to domestic credit causes EMP to increase (decrease) by about 1.4 percent. Note that an estimate of unity lies within two standard errors. As a numerical example, with a monetary base equal to US$1.6 billion (the average for 1998), a US$16 million reduction (expansion) of central bank domestic assets implies an approximate US$20 million rise (fall) in international reserves (with a fixed exchange rate). Traditional monetary models suggest that international reserves would rise (fall) by US$16 million, and this amount lies within the confidence interval.

[108]An IRF is significant if its t-statistic exceeds |2|.

In subsequent periods, effects of w_δ on EMP remain positive, but with t-statistics below 2. Between months 0 and 5, the cumulative response of a 1 percent increase (decrease) to δ is an increase (decrease) in EMP of about 3¾ percent.

Positive shocks to changes in the interest rate differential (w_ϕ) negatively affect EMP (see Table 35, part B, and Figure 14, bottom). The hypothesis that lagged $\Delta\phi$ does not help explain why current EMP is rejected at slightly higher than the 95 percent confidence level. There is an IRF at month 3 that is negative and significant. That is, according to these results, a 1 percent positive (negative) shock to the change in the interest rate differential causes EMP to fall (rise) by about 1 percent, but after three months.

Shocks to EMP (w_E) positively affect $\Delta\phi$ (see Table 35, part B and Figure 15, top). A positive relationship between w_E and $\Delta\phi$ should not be surprising, as higher (lower) EMP generally indicates higher (lower) expected exchange rate depreciation, risk, or both. Reduced (increased) EMP boosts (lowers) investor confidence and reduces (increases) the domestic interest rate (relative to its U.S. counterpart). The hypothesis that EMP does not help explain current $\Delta\phi$ is rejected only at the 80 percent level (as shown in Table 35, Part B). The response, however, of $\Delta\phi$ to a shock to EMP after two months equals 0.3 and has a t-statistic of about 2.19. That is, a 1 percent reduction (increase) in EMP reduces (increases) the interest rate differential by about 30 basis points after two months.

Domestic credit shocks (w_δ) appear to have little effect on the change in interest rate differentials (see Table 35, bottom and Figure 15, bottom). Such a finding need not be surprising, given the theoretically ambiguous nature of the link between these two variables, as mentioned in the previous section. The hypothesis that lagged δ does not help explain current ϕ is not rejected at conventional levels, and there are no significant responses.

Regarding a policy reaction function, there is little evidence that EMP shocks (w_E) systematically affect the growth of domestic credit (δ) (see Table 35, bottom and Figure 16, top). The hypothesis that lagged

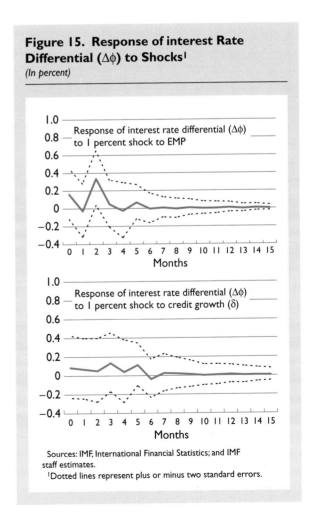

Figure 14. Response of EMP to Shocks[1]
(In percent)

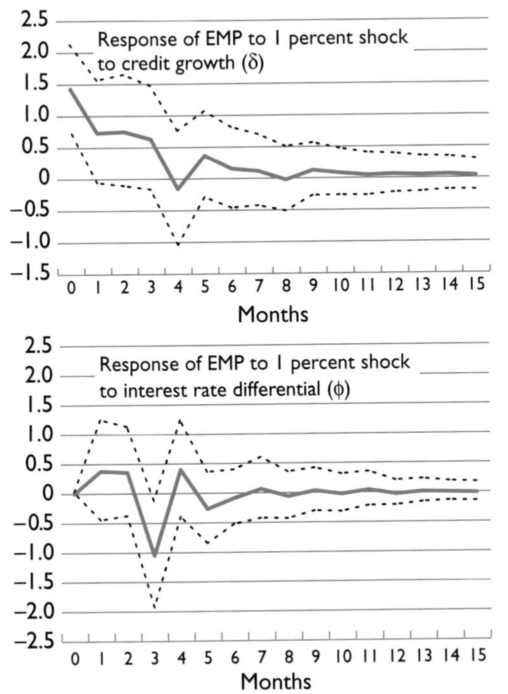

Response of EMP to 1 percent shock to credit growth (δ)

Response of EMP to 1 percent shock to interest rate differential (ϕ)

Sources: IMF, International Financial Statistics; and IMF staff estimates.
[1]Dotted lines represent plus or minus two standard errors.

Figure 15. Response of interest Rate Differential ($\Delta\phi$) to Shocks[1]
(In percent)

Response of interest rate differential ($\Delta\phi$) to 1 percent shock to EMP

Response of interest rate differential ($\Delta\phi$) to 1 percent shock to credit growth (δ)

Sources: IMF, International Financial Statistics; and IMF staff estimates.
[1]Dotted lines represent plus or minus two standard errors.

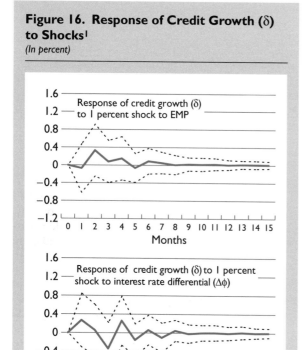

Figure 16. Response of Credit Growth (δ) to Shocks[1]

(In percent)

Sources: IMF, International Financial Statistics; and IMF staff estimates.

[1]Dotted lines represent plus or minus two standard errors.

EMP does not help explain current δ is not rejected at conventional levels. Moreover, no IRF has a t-statistic exceeding |2|. This suggests that the authorities have not been forced to respond, on average, to increased EMP with additional liquidity to the banking system.[109]

Likewise, there is little evidence linking shocks to the interest rate differential (w_ϕ) to δ (see Table 35 and Figure 16, bottom). Rather, the hypothesis that lagged $\Delta\phi$ does not help explain current δ is not rejected at conventional levels, and there are no significant responses.

Summary and Policy Implications

This chapter examined the relationship between EMP and monetary policy during the 1990s. Since the exchange rate regime was neither perfectly fixed nor freely floating, it would be misleading to focus exclusively on either reserve or exchange rate movements. Rather, EMP is more appropriate as it summarizes the difference between the growth rates of money supply and demand under managed exchange rate regimes.

This chapter provided evidence on several questions. First, shocks to the domestic credit component of the monetary base have powerful impacts on EMP in the "right" direction: a reduction in δ helps reduce EMP (either by increasing the value of the peso or the stock of international reserves, or both). The response of EMP to interest shocks was somewhat weaker than that linking EMP and domestic credit growth, but also in the "right" direction. These findings, taken together, support the hypothesis that monetary policy is effective in controlling EMP. In a related vein, the chapter provided some insights into the determinants of interest rate differentials, that is, that shocks to EMP positively affect interest rate differentials. This is to be expected, since higher EMP signals both expected exchange rate depreciation and higher risk.

This chapter has three main policy implications. First, the stance of monetary policy, as measured by the growth of the net domestic assets of the central bank (δ), has been an important determinant of EMP. On a contemporaneous basis alone, the growth of central bank domestic assets explains about 17 percent of all movements in EMP. Second, monetary policy is effective in helping to build up reserves. According to the estimates, a 1 percent reduction in the net domestic assets of the central bank will increase reserves (reduce EMP) in the same period by about 1.4 percent. In subsequent periods, there should be additional reserve gains. Numerically, with a monetary base equal to US\$1.6 billion (the average for 1998), a US\$16 million reduction of central bank domestic assets implies an approximate US\$20 million increase in international reserves.[110] Third, EMP (primarily reserve movements in the case of the Dominican Republic) feed back to the interest rate differential. The estimates suggest that a US\$16 million increase in reserves will reduce the spread between domestic and U.S. interest rates by about 30 basis points.

References

Bernanke, Ben, 1986, "Alternative Explanations of the Money-Income Correlation," in K. Brunner and A. Meltzer, eds., *Real Business Cycles, Real Exchange*

---

[109]Tanner (2001) finds strong responses of δ to EMP within two months for Indonesia, Korea, Thailand, and Mexico. For a discussion of such behavior for balance of payments crises, see Flood, Garber, and Kramer (1996).

---

[110]Such a reduction might reflect a corresponding reduction in the government budget deficit.

Rates, and Actual Policies, Carnegie Rochester Series on Public Policy No. 25.

————, and Alan Blinder, 1992, "The Federal Funds Rate and the Channels of Monetary Transmission," *American Economic Review,* Vol. 82, pp. 901–21.

————, and Ilian Mihov, 1998, "Measuring Monetary Policy," *Quarterly Journal of Economics,* Vol. 3 (August), Vol. 113, pp. 869–902.

Brissimis, Sophocles N., and John A. Leventakis, 1984, "An Empirical Inquiry into the Short-Run Dynamics of Output, Prices and Exchange Market Pressure," *Journal of International Money and Finance,* Vol. 3, pp. 75–89.

Burkett, Paul, and Donald G. Richards, 1993, "Exchange Market Pressure in Paraguay, 1963–88: Monetary Disequilibrium Versus Global and Regional Dependency," *Applied Economics,* Vol. 25, pp. 1053–63.

Calvo, Guillermo, and Enrique Mendoza, 1996, "Mexico's Balance-of-Payments Crisis: A Chronicle of a Death Foretold," *Journal of International Economics,* Vol. 41, pp. 235–64.

Christiano, Lawrence, Martin Eichenbaum, and Charles Evans, 1998, "Monetary Policy Shocks: What Have We Learned and To What End?" National Bureau of Economic Research, Working Paper 6400, February.

Connolly, Michael, and Jose Dantas da Silveira, 1979, "Exchange Market Pressure in Postwar Brazil: An Application of the Girton-Roper Monetary Model," *American Economic Review,* Vol. 69, pp. 448–54.

Edwards, Sebastian, and Miguel Savastano, 1998, "The Morning After: The Mexican Peso in the Aftermath of the 1994 Currency Crisis," National Bureau of Economic Research, Working Paper 6516.

Eichengreen, Barry, Andrew Rose, and Charles Wyplosz, 1996, "Contagious Currency Crises: First Tests," *Scandinavian Journal of Economics,* 98, 4, pp. 463–84.

Enders, Walter, 1995, *Applied Econometric Time Series* (New York: John Wiley and Sons).

Flood, Robert, Peter Garber, and Charles Kramer, 1996, "Collapsing Exchange Rate Regimes: Another Linear Example," *Journal of International Economics,* Vol. 41, pp. 223–34.

Furman, Jason, and Joseph Stiglitz, 1998, "Economic Crises: Evidence and Insights from East Asia," *Brookings Papers on Economic Activity,* Vol. 0, pp. 1–114 (Washington: World Bank).

Girton, Lance, and Don Roper, 1977, "A Monetary Model of Exchange Market Pressure Applied to the Postwar Canadian Experience," *American Economic Review,* Vol. 67, pp. 537–48.

Goldfajn, Ilan, and Taimur Baig, 1998, "Monetary Policy in the Aftermath of Currency Crises: The Case of Asia," Working Paper WP/98/170 (Washington: International Monetary Fund).

Goldfajn, Ilan, and Poonam Gupta, 1998, "Does Tight Monetary Policy Stabilize the Exchange Rate Following a Currency Crisis?" Working Paper WP/99/42 (Washington: International Monetary Fund).

Kaminsky, Graciela, Saul Lizondo, and Carmen M. Reinhart, 1998, "Leading Indicators of Currency Crises," *IMF Staff Papers,* Vol. 45, pp. 1–48.

Radelet, Steven, and Jeffery D. Sachs, 1998, "The East Asian Financial Crisis: Diagnoses, Remedies, Prospects," *Brookings Papers on Economic Activity,* Vol. 0, pp. 1–74.

Tanner, Evan, 2001, "Exchange Market Pressure and Monetary Policy: Asia and Latin America in the 1990s," *IMF Staff Papers,* Vol. 47, pp. 311–33 (Washington: International Monetary Fund).

Weymark, Diana N., 1995, "Estimating Exchange Market Pressure and the Degree of Exchange Market Intervention for Canada," *Journal of International Economics,* Vol. 39, pp. 273–95.

————, 1998, "A General Approach to Measuring Exchange Market Pressure," *Oxford Economic Papers,* Vol. 50, pp. 106–21.

Wohar, Mark E., and Bun Song Lee, 1992, "Application of the Girton-Roper Monetary Model of Exchange Market Pressure: The Japanese Experience, 1959–1991," *Rivista Internazionale di Scienze Economiche e Commerciali,* Vol. 39, 12 (December); pp. 993–1013.

Recent Occasional Papers of the International Monetary Fund

207. Malaysia: From Crisis to Recovery, by Kanitta Meesook, Il Houng Lee, Olin Liu, Yougesh Khatri, Natalia Tamirisa, Michael Moore, and Mark H. Krysl. 2001.

206. The Dominican Republic: Stabilization, Structural Reform, and Economic Growth, by Alessandro Giustiniani, Werner C. Keller, and Randa E. Sab. 2001

205. Stabilization and Savings Funds for Nonrenewable Resources, by Jeffrey Davis, Rolando Ossowski, James Daniel, and Steven Barnett. 2001.

204. Monetary Union in West Africa (ECOWAS): Is It Desirable and How Could It Be Achieved? by Paul Masson and Catherine Pattillo. 2001.

203. Modern Banking and OTC Derivatives Markets: The Transformation of Global Finance and Its Implications for Systemic Risk, by Garry J. Schinasi, R. Sean Craig, Burkhard Drees, and Charles Kramer. 2000.

202. Adopting Inflation Targeting: Practical Issues for Emerging Market Countries, by Andrea Schaechter, Mark R. Stone, and Mark Zelmer. 2000.

201. Developments and Challenges in the Caribbean Region, by Samuel Itam, Simon Cueva, Erik Lundback, Janet Stotsky, and Stephen Tokarick. 2000.

200. Pension Reform in the Baltics: Issues and Prospects, by Jerald Schiff, Niko Hobdari, Axel Schimmelpfennig, and Roman Zytek. 2000.

199. Ghana: Economic Development in a Democratic Environment, by Sérgio Pereira Leite, Anthony Pellechio, Luisa Zanforlin, Girma Begashaw, Stefania Fabrizio, and Joachim Harnack. 2000.

198. Setting Up Treasuries in the Baltics, Russia, and Other Countries of the Former Soviet Union: An Assessment of IMF Technical Assistance, by Barry H. Potter and Jack Diamond. 2000.

197. Deposit Insurance: Actual and Good Practices, by Gillian G.H. Garcia. 2000.

196. Trade and Trade Policies in Eastern and Southern Africa, by a staff team led by Arvind Subramanian, with Enrique Gelbard, Richard Harmsen, Katrin Elborgh-Woytek, and Piroska Nagy. 2000.

195. The Eastern Caribbean Currency Union—Institutions, Performance, and Policy Issues, by Frits van Beek, José Roberto Rosales, Mayra Zermeño, Ruby Randall, and Jorge Shepherd. 2000.

194. Fiscal and Macroeconomic Impact of Privatization, by Jeffrey Davis, Rolando Ossowski, Thomas Richardson, and Steven Barnett. 2000.

193. Exchange Rate Regimes in an Increasingly Integrated World Economy, by Michael Mussa, Paul Masson, Alexander Swoboda, Esteban Jadresic, Paolo Mauro, and Andy Berg. 2000.

192. Macroprudential Indicators of Financial System Soundness, by a staff team led by Owen Evans, Alfredo M. Leone, Mahinder Gill, and Paul Hilbers. 2000.

191. Social Issues in IMF-Supported Programs, by Sanjeev Gupta, Louis Dicks-Mireaux, Ritha Khemani, Calvin McDonald, and Marijn Verhoeven. 2000.

190. Capital Controls: Country Experiences with Their Use and Liberalization, by Akira Ariyoshi, Karl Habermeier, Bernard Laurens, Inci Ötker-Robe, Jorge Iván Canales Kriljenko, and Andrei Kirilenko. 2000.

189. Current Account and External Sustainability in the Baltics, Russia, and Other Countries of the Former Soviet Union, by Donal McGettigan. 2000.

188. Financial Sector Crisis and Restructuring: Lessons from Asia, by Carl-Johan Lindgren, Tomás J.T. Baliño, Charles Enoch, Anne-Marie Gulde, Marc Quintyn, and Leslie Teo. 1999.

187. Philippines: Toward Sustainable and Rapid Growth, Recent Developments and the Agenda Ahead, by Markus Rodlauer, Prakash Loungani, Vivek Arora, Charalambos Christofides, Enrique G. De la Piedra, Piyabha Kongsamut, Kristina Kostial, Victoria Summers, and Athanasios Vamvakidis. 2000.

186. Anticipating Balance of Payments Crises: The Role of Early Warning Systems, by Andrew Berg, Eduardo Borensztein, Gian Maria Milesi-Ferretti, and Catherine Pattillo. 1999.

185. Oman Beyond the Oil Horizon: Policies Toward Sustainable Growth, edited by Ahsan Mansur and Volker Treichel. 1999.

184. Growth Experience in Transition Countries, 1990–98, by Oleh Havrylyshyn, Thomas Wolf, Julian Berengaut, Marta Castello-Branco, Ron van Rooden, and Valerie Mercer-Blackman. 1999.

183. Economic Reforms in Kazakhstan, Kyrgyz Republic, Tajikistan, Turkmenistan, and Uzbekistan, by Emine Gürgen, Harry Snoek, Jon Craig, Jimmy McHugh, Ivailo Izvorski, and Ron van Rooden. 1999.

182. Tax Reform in the Baltics, Russia, and Other Countries of the Former Soviet Union, by a staff team led by Liam Ebrill and Oleh Havrylyshyn. 1999.

181. The Netherlands: Transforming a Market Economy, by C. Maxwell Watson, Bas B. Bakker, Jan Kees Martijn, and Ioannis Halikias. 1999.

180. Revenue Implications of Trade Liberalization, by Liam Ebrill, Janet Stotsky, and Reint Gropp. 1999.

179. Disinflation in Transition: 1993–97, by Carlo Cottarelli and Peter Doyle. 1999.

178. IMF-Supported Programs in Indonesia, Korea, and Thailand: A Preliminary Assessment, by Timothy Lane, Atish Ghosh, Javier Hamann, Steven Phillips, Marianne Schulze-Ghattas, and Tsidi Tsikata. 1999.

177. Perspectives on Regional Unemployment in Europe, by Paolo Mauro, Eswar Prasad, and Antonio Spilimbergo. 1999.

176. Back to the Future: Postwar Reconstruction and Stabilization in Lebanon, edited by Sena Eken and Thomas Helbling. 1999.

175. Macroeconomic Developments in the Baltics, Russia, and Other Countries of the Former Soviet Union, 1992–97, by Luis M. Valdivieso. 1998.

174. Impact of EMU on Selected Non–European Union Countries, by R. Feldman, K. Nashashibi, R. Nord, P. Allum, D. Desruelle, K. Enders, R. Kahn, and H. Temprano-Arroyo. 1998.

173. The Baltic Countries: From Economic Stabilization to EU Accession, by Julian Berengaut, Augusto Lopez-Claros, Françoise Le Gall, Dennis Jones, Richard Stern, Ann-Margret Westin, Effie Psalida, Pietro Garibaldi. 1998.

172. Capital Account Liberalization: Theoretical and Practical Aspects, by a staff team led by Barry Eichengreen and Michael Mussa, with Giovanni Dell'Ariccia, Enrica Detragiache, Gian Maria Milesi-Ferretti, and Andrew Tweedie. 1998.

171. Monetary Policy in Dollarized Economies, by Tomás Baliño, Adam Bennett, and Eduardo Borensztein. 1998.

170. The West African Economic and Monetary Union: Recent Developments and Policy Issues, by a staff team led by Ernesto Hernández-Catá and comprising Christian A. François, Paul Masson, Pascal Bouvier, Patrick Peroz, Dominique Desruelle, and Athanasios Vamvakidis. 1998.

169. Financial Sector Development in Sub-Saharan African Countries, by Hassanali Mehran, Piero Ugolini, Jean Phillipe Briffaux, George Iden, Tonny Lybek, Stephen Swaray, and Peter Hayward. 1998.

168. Exit Strategies: Policy Options for Countries Seeking Greater Exchange Rate Flexibility, by a staff team led by Barry Eichengreen and Paul Masson with Hugh Bredenkamp, Barry Johnston, Javier Hamann, Esteban Jadresic, and Inci Ötker. 1998.

167. Exchange Rate Assessment: Extensions of the Macroeconomic Balance Approach, edited by Peter Isard and Hamid Faruqee. 1998

166. Hedge Funds and Financial Market Dynamics, by a staff team led by Barry Eichengreen and Donald Mathieson with Bankim Chadha, Anne Jansen, Laura Kodres, and Sunil Sharma. 1998.

165. Algeria: Stabilization and Transition to the Market, by Karim Nashashibi, Patricia Alonso-Gamo, Stefania Bazzoni, Alain Féler, Nicole Laframboise, and Sebastian Paris Horvitz. 1998.

164. MULTIMOD Mark III: The Core Dynamic and Steady-State Model, by Douglas Laxton, Peter Isard, Hamid Faruqee, Eswar Prasad, and Bart Turtelboom. 1998.

163. Egypt: Beyond Stabilization, Toward a Dynamic Market Economy, by a staff team led by Howard Handy. 1998.

Note: For information on the title and availability of Occasional Papers not listed, please consult the IMF Publications Catalog or contact IMF Publication Services.